Intersex
(For Lack of A Better Word)

~ Also by Thea Hillman ~

Depending on the Light

Intersex
(For Lack of A Better Word)

Thea Hillman

Manic D Press
San Francisco

Grateful acknowledgement is made to the following publications where some of these pieces originally appeared in a slightly different form:

Full Zine #2, Pants on Fire: Secrets and Lies; Love, Castro Street: Reflections on San Francisco (Alyson); *On Our Backs* Vol. 19 #3; *Pills, Thrills, Chills, and Heartache: Adventures in the First Person* (Alyson); and *Cometbus #49*

Cover photographs: Tadija Savic / Yegor Piaskovsky

Library of Congress Cataloging-in-Publication Data

Hillman, Thea, 1971-
    Intersex (for lack of a better word) / Thea Hillman.
       p. cm.
    ISBN 978-1-933149-24-0 (trade pbk. original)
    1. Hillman, Thea, 1971- 2. Intersex people--California--Biography.
    I. Title.
    RC883.H55 2008
    616.6'940092--dc22
    [B]
                                        2008031663

for You
the ones who make room in the world for each of us

and for
Kris Kovick, Laura Trent, and David Reimer

Contents

Haircut

I don't know what we were doing. I think we had just come home from a successful trip to Target, successful meaning not too much money spent and no meltdown on either of our parts, and we were rolling around on my bed, making out, laughing, and she said, "Hey, I have an idea. Let me give you a haircut."

She wanted to give me a haircut. Down there. She thought it would be hot.

What I should have told her right then is that I'm kind of sensitive about my hair down there. That it's been there since I was a toddler, that it makes me feel special, and that I'm still ashamed of it even though most people have caught up with me by this point and have pubic hair too. I should have told her that somehow I always end up with hairless girls; no matter how butch they are, I'm always hairier than them. And that sometimes this makes me feel less than pretty. Of course, since testosterone has come into our community, that's changed, but I didn't say that either.

Instead I said, "Sure."

I handed her the scissors from the bathroom cabinet. The haircutting scissors I stole from my dad when I was a kid, stolen as only a well-loved child can, my parents' possessions mine for the taking, a birthright. These scissors are the kind with teeth so sharp they seem to cut molecules of air as they close. Like a surgical implement, they're long, thin, silver, and cold.

She wanted me to lie down on the bathroom floor so she could get a better angle.

There was one lover whose hands I jumped away from the whole time we were together. I didn't mean to. I couldn't help it. We had amazing sex together—I certainly enjoyed it—but most often it was amazing for her. I couldn't relax. I couldn't trust her hands.

I did not want to lie down on the bathroom floor, even though my girlfriend asked nicely. I sat on the toilet.

Right before that lover whose hands I jumped from and I broke up, she had a dream about one of my best friends. Someone who is very beautiful, someone she kissed once. That lover told me, "I dreamed about your friend last night, that I was making love to her, and that she wasn't ticklish, and that she didn't jerk away like you did." I told her I was sorry. I told her that it must be painful to feel you can't touch your lover right.

I think the ticklishness started with the doctors. Well, one doctor, whose job it was to make sure I was developing at a normal rate, whose fingers pushed on my chest to see if breast tissue was developing, whose fingers opened me to make sure my clitoris was doing everything it was supposed to and not one bit more.

It was cold sitting there, watching the scissors do their work, and I was getting more nervous by the minute, the ice cold of the metal biting my skin. "Be careful," I said. "I'm scared," I said. "I'm not sure that's a good angle either," I said. The sharp scissor tips were poking my labia. I was beginning to panic, but I wanted to give her what she wanted, so I let her keep going.

Years of having sex with women, or people who were designated as female at birth, has taught me a lot about having sex with survivors of sexual abuse. I recognize the stillness of someone leaving their body. I know that one lover might want to be choked, while another will say, "Never touch my throat." Another talks nasty, but you can never use the word dirty with her. Another likes to be hit, but never on the face because that's where he hit her. One only likes it on her back, while another only on top. The older I get, the more amazing I think it is that we share our bodies with each other, that we risk vulnerability again and again. The older I get, the more I follow the legends of these complicated maps, the more I appreciate the sacred ground I'm treading on.

She's on the bathroom floor, I'm sitting on the toilet, and even though she doesn't know it, she's totally in control. I'm reduced to feeling like a small child, and even though I'm petrified, I'm committed to letting her be in charge. I'm trying so hard to give it up.

And then she cuts me. The scissors slice my flesh, just a little bit, but it's everything. And then she says she needs to stop. Then she starts to cry. And then she leaves the room. She leaves me sitting there, naked on the toilet.

My mind races. I can barely grasp the fact that I am the naked one, scared and vulnerable, and that she's crying. It makes no sense to me.

The more I learn the secrets of other people's bodies, the more patient I am when they need to stop, slow down, the more I realize I haven't said "No" very often. That I apologize for being ticklish instead of listening to what it's telling me. That I need to teach people how to touch me so my body will trust them, that my body is smarter and wiser than I am. That maybe it realizes there's a survivor in many of us, or at least in me.

I am learning that being comfortable with sex doesn't mean sex is comfortable, and that not being ashamed of sex doesn't mean there aren't layers of shame hiding in there, invisible to my eye, places I've never seen, in the dark recesses, where only the sharp, cool tools of a doctor have been.

Funny

My mom pulled out a copy of *The Onion* today. "There's something I've been meaning to show you," she says, holding up the paper for me to see the headline: Poverty Stricken Africans To Receive Desperately Needed Bibles.

"Mom, that's fake. It's a joke," I answer, and she starts laughing hard. We're having a quick coffee before she goes her brunch date with a man she's met online. We scan a few more pages together. My favorite headline: captives, captor have different senses of humor.

The thing about humor is, sometimes it's universal, and sometimes it's just the most personal thing in the world. Sometimes when I hear what makes someone laugh, I almost can't look them in the eye because I feel like I just saw through to their inner workings, and I'm not even sure they just meant to show me everything: the levers, cranks, pulleys, and switches. It's the girl falling out of her top, accidentally flashing anatomy. She might not even be ashamed, but I am, for her. And then there's laughing itself, the mouth so open, a moment unplanned, when you can tell just how tightly someone's wound.

I had a favorite joke when I was little. I don't remember when I first heard it, but I remember the first time I told it. I was in fourth grade, hanging out after school with one or two other kids, telling stories on an upper platform of the red play structure, high above the yard, the teachers, the younger kids.

"A woman goes to the doctor," I start. My voice then climbs up to approximate a woman's: " 'Doctor, those hormone pills you're giving me are really just too strong.'

" 'How can you tell?' he asks.

" 'I have hair on my chest.'

" 'How far down does it go?' he asks.

" 'Down to my balls, and that's another thing I wanted to tell you about.' "

I'm pretty sure I got a good response from the kids for this joke. If nothing else, the word balls is always good for a laugh. I remember how I felt telling this joke: mature, like I had something on the other kids, some privileged information about what adult bodies are like; and naughty, like I knew something I wasn't supposed to know, some privileged information about what adult bodies are like.

I don't actually think the joke is funny. But it makes me wonder what I was doing telling this joke, what kind of information I was trying to give these kids about me, about my body, without flashing anatomy or telling them something they didn't ask about or want to know.

Special

My mother helps me dress, pulling up the heavy cloth underwear around my thick little legs. She looks at my child's body and at the same time doesn't look, like a mother with two toddlers and food on the stove who's late for the carpool does, noticing everything and nothing at the same time. We are singing the song about the muffin man. Do you know the muffin man, the muffin man, the muffin man, do you know the muffin man that lives on Drury Lane? And then she sees—a shadow? She stops pulling up the underwear, stops singing, and looks closer. Her breathing stops. Her fingers tighten around the white fabric. Several tiny hairs, but thick. And dark. I'm wriggling, and ask, "Why aren't you singing, Mommy?" My mother looks up, sees me watching her, and quickly wipes the horror from her face. She smiles and continues dressing me, trying to hide her panic.

My mother's first frantic thought is, Oh, my God, my daughter's got Virilizing Adrenal Hyperplasia. I know, it couldn't sound weirder if I made it up. But I didn't. It's an unlikely thought, yes, but a wildly coincidental twist of fate that only real life could come up with. At four years old I'm growing pubic hair and my mother is reminded of Paul, that problem child who was in her class when she was teaching second grade in Canada. Paul had facial and pubic hair at age eight. Throughout the whole school year, his mother would talk to my mom, telling her about the search to find out what was going on with this precocious, hyperactive boy with behavior problems. Mom remembers when he was finally diagnosed: the mother told her Paul had Virilizing Adrenal Hyperplasia. And that he was going to be very short. She remembers that Paul often got very angry and uncharacteristically tense. And it's that similar behavior in me that helps her make the connection.

There are moments when she doesn't recognize her sweet baby.

Especially when I'm crying. My little fists ball up and my legs kick, pushing away at diapers, blankets, or comforting hands. There's a tension, an out-of-control quality to my crying, a fitful anxiety that can't be soothed or rocked away. For Mom, it's as if her daughter has been replaced by an angry, screaming other. It's been happening for quite a while now, since I was two, she says. It's not colic, because I had colic as a newborn. This is different.

When my father gets home from the office that night, my mother takes him into the kitchen so that my brother Jonah and I, playing in the den, won't hear what she has to say. When he hears of her discovery, my father isn't all that concerned. I'm healthy, after all, and everything else looks fine. Plus, I'm the smartest kid around, he says. This whole parenting thing, especially babies and little kids, is new to my dad. When I was just three days old, he took me for a walk in the baby carrier, snug against his chest. I slept the whole time, he likes to say— that is, until he stopped by Swenson's for a licorice ice cream cone for us to share. "You loved it!" he says. "Your little pink tongue kept poking out for more." By the time we arrived home, Mom was greeted by her proud husband and her newborn, my brand-new little face completely covered with black ice cream.

She takes me to the pediatrician. She tells him what she thinks is wrong. He does a thorough examination, orders a couple of tests. My mother takes me to the hospital to get a blood test. I go back to preschool the next day and tell everyone that I had a blood test and I didn't even cry. I tell them getting a blood test is better than going to the dentist. The test results come back. Some things are a little low, others a little high, the doctor says. He can't find anything wrong. He tells my mom, "I wouldn't worry if I were you." Easy for you to say, she thinks. And wonders if she's crazy. And also where to take me next.

She decides to take me to her endocrinologist, whom she had been seeing for her high cholesterol. She waits with me for an hour in the bland waiting room, feeling stupid and wondering if she should just take me home. There's nothing for me to play with, not even a Highlights magazine, and I'm bored.

After a nurse measures my weight and height, we're ushered into the examination room. "I know I'm throwing my money away," Mom says to her endocrinologist. "But why does my four-year-old child have pubic hair?" The doctor is a kind man, and shy. He has dark hair, a big mustache, and thick glasses that make his eyes big and round, like fish eyes. He's so tall that he bends a bit like a tree that sways, except that he's often still, curved over the notebook that he writes everything in.

The examination table is for grownups and Mom has to lift me onto it. The doctor does a quick physical examination, his large hands palpating my chest to check for breast development, pressing my belly, and then pulling down my underwear, noting the pubic hair, and pulling my labia apart to see if there's clitoral enlargement, which there isn't. He's not used to working with kids, but he jokes with me, trying to put me at ease. He seems embarrassed and performs his examination as fast as he can. I'm embarrassed, too, and ticklish under his cold hands. I'm glad when he's done and Mom takes me down from the table.

The doctor agrees to take me on as a patient even though he's really an endocrinologist for adults. He orders a battery of tests. My mother takes me for countless blood tests, bone age tests, and so many other tests that my mother has long since forgotten their names and their purposes. I sit in the little desk for the blood test, kind of like the chairs at Baskin Robin's, but with a swiveling table to put my arm on. I'm not very scared and am always interested to know how many tubes of blood the lady is going to take. They are always women. One time, after a lady took four tubes, she took Mom and me into the lab to see the machines that process the blood. The machines were big, with see-through tubes of blood running through them. I couldn't concentrate because I got nauseous suddenly from all the blood they took and couldn't figure out why everything had purple spots on it.

We go for test after test for close to six months, and each test makes my mother more nervous. With every one, she has to consider a whole new set of terrifying outcomes and treatments. I'm tested for genetic disorders, birth defects, hormonal imbalances—and each offers a different, bleak future of illness, drug treatments, and discomfort. I don't mind the blood tests, even though I have to not eat the night before and morning of the tests. Usually we go out for breakfast after.

I get to eat an omelet, or maybe even a donut on my way to school. I feel important missing school to go to a hospital or lab for the tests. I now know the word phlebotomist. Everyone is really nice to me and I like all the attention. Over the course of the several months it takes the doctor to analyze and piece together test results, my mom goes to the local medical library to research hormonal disorders, particularly Virilizing Adrenal Hyperplasia. This is before computers, so she studies from medical books. She devours these books, looking for answers. And what she finds is horrifying.

Each book is filled with pictures of naked children, their eyes blackened out. Children with strange-looking genitals, their bodies vulnerable and small, captured on the pages, victims of harsh light, the extreme close-up, and a complete lack of consideration for the young human inside the body. The pictures that scare her the most are the pictures of the girls with excess virilizing hormones, the girls that I might grow up to be like, the girls who are dwarfs, who have full beards. Most of these girls stare straight into the camera, every single one miserable. And then there are the words: disorder, masculinized, hermaphrodism, cliteromegaly, abnormal.

Mom picks me and my brother up from day care and preschool after looking at these pictures, petrified beyond belief, full of terror. And shame. And guilt. She is wracked with questions, wondering what she's done to cause this: Was it smoking cigarettes? (But we didn't know better then.) Smoking marijuana? Being Canadian? She tells people about the doctor's appointments, but that's all.

Eventually, Mom stops telling Dad about the tests and about how scared she is. She feels neurotic and alone. She doesn't tell anyone her fears: that I might not grow up normally, that I might be a dwarf, or grow a beard, or something else unimaginable. She bathes me and sees my little hairs, and her fears clutch her. And she thinks, My poor sweetie, poor little girl.

One by one the tests come back and a picture emerges. My bone age is advanced, meaning that I'm growing too fast for my age. And I have high levels of androgens—hormones that are speeding up my growth and development process. My mom had been right. It looks like I do indeed have Congenital Adrenal Hyperplasia, called CAH for short. The doctor tells my mom that since it was detected so early, there is a chance to get me back on track. With close supervision and monitoring of my hormone levels through regular blood tests, they can try to stave off puberty. And if it is successful, I will reach a short-to-normal height, will begin my puberty at a normal age, and won't have excess facial and body hair.

Vindicated and armed with some information, my mom goes about trying to find out how to treat my condition. No one knows for sure. Many more blood tests and visits to doctors ensue. A woman doctor discovers that my case of CAH is very slight, enough so to be called borderline. Since it isn't full-blown, my case had been harder to detect, but also would probably have much milder effects.

My mother tells me about the diagnosis. She tells me I have an imbalance. And that I have to wear a medic alert bracelet. I love jewelry and find this news very exciting. She tells me I'll have to have a lot of blood tests and that I'll have to take medication, maybe for the rest of my life. I think this makes me very grown up, because adults take pills, especially my grandparents, who line them up beside their glass of orange juice each morning. She tells me about periods, and that I might get mine early. I can't wait. She tells me that I won't have more pubic hair than anyone else, just that I got mine earlier. I love the idea that I have something other kids don't. I decide this makes me special.

What she doesn't tell me is that CAH is a condition that can result in hermaphrodism in girls. This usually reveals itself with an enlarged clitoris and precocious puberty, which can result in shortened stature, masculinization, and other effects including inability to get pregnant. She doesn't tell me that CAH speeds up brain maturity, or that she worries about me being socially advanced beyond my peers and the hardships that might cause. She doesn't tell me many of the girls with CAH end up being bisexual or lesbian, or that she's concerned about the possibility of me being very sexual because of the increased androgens running through me. It's not that I think she should have told me these things. It's just that they were there, between us and around me, hovering behind every word and gesture.

Pray

You and I have bodies that make people pray.

Your fingers, simultaneously curled and pointing, as if arguing a complicated point or eternally on the edge of an exquisitely slow orgasm.

Please God, your mother said, I'll do anything to make this go away.

My child body, twisting with unexplained rage, sprouting pubic hair before kindergarten, threatening precocious puberty for years, a storm cloud constantly about to burst.

Oh God, my mother said, please make my daughter normal.

Praying for salvation. Making deals with the devil.

We met at a disability conference. We met at a spoken word event in DC. We met at Fairybutch. You liked my work. I liked your shoes. We liked each other immediately.

You send a mass email to the attendees of a queer conference in a foreign country asking for help from strangers. To go to the bathroom. I find out later you happen to be on your period. As I'm driving to the conference with a friend of mine, she tells me she knows I will be one of the people to answer that call. And she's right.

We must be able to lift forty pounds and set aside forty-five minutes. I find out later I can barely lift forty pounds. In an act that's intensely intimate for me and absolutely routine for you, a transwoman and I work together with you in the bathroom. While she lifts your torso, I slide your underwear down over your hips and legs. But that's not true; there's not a lot of sliding when it comes to removing your underwear; there is tugging and inching and shifting and pulling. My friend says she knew I would help you at the conference, because that's the kind of thing I do.

I have always been close with people who use wheelchairs, crutches, and canes. I used to wonder if I just wanted to look good, to God or whoever else was watching. After all, I had a normal body.

Oh God, says my co-worker, when she pulls me aside after she interviews a potential employee who uses a wheelchair. I knew I could tell you this, she says. I knew you'd understand. See, my first thought, she says, was God, don't make me deal with this. The bargain.

I build muscle too easily, you with too much effort, arms hard and strong from the constant workout of walking.

We're friends because we recognize each other. Just as my trans lovers reflect my outwardly simple though visually misleading, internally complicated gender, you outwardly reflect my externally simple though visually misleading, internally complicated chemistry. Your twisted calf: the shape of my hormone imbalance. Your spastic muscles: my renegade enzymes charting undecipherable pathways.

Your mother prayed you wouldn't fall.

My mother prayed I wouldn't be gay (although I bet your mother prayed for that one too).

We have fallen so many times. Fallen short, fallen behind, fallen, and then more or less grown up.

You and you and you and I are our mothers' worst nightmares.

And yet they thank God each day for our perfection.

Developing

I get taken for blood tests often. I go to summer school. And to swim classes. Mom waits by the side of the pool and talks to other mothers during the class. I've been swimming since I was nine months old. One of those classes where mommies and babies swim together, classes that start out by just tossing the baby in the water. At the swim classes at the woman's house, we learn to blow bubbles and hold our breath when our heads are under the water.

During one of these swim classes, I happen to be in the middle of taking a urine test. It's a twenty-four-hour urine test in which every bit of my pee needs to be collected, labeled with the time and date, and then brought to a lab all together. The doctor needs to see how much of certain chemicals my body produces and at what times, so that we can then mimic that with medication. I have to pee into little cups. I'm surprised at how small the cups are, sure that my pee is going to overflow them, because sometimes when I pee it just seems to go on forever, but it never does overflow the containers. My parents follow me like hawks, knowing that I am too young to remember not to pee in the toilet. Before the swim class, my mom tells me, "Now, Thea, don't pee in the pool." I love the swim class and of course drink lots of chlorinated water, and before I know it, I start peeing in the warm pool. I yell over to my mom while I'm peeing, "Mom, I'm going..." as if I could stop, as if maybe it isn't quite so bad if I tell her while I'm doing it that I'm ruining eighteen hours of urine collection. She says, "Oh, Thea!" but it's already too late, there's nothing we can do, and I can tell from her voice that she's exasperated but I won't get in trouble. We start all over again, and this time I remember. We drop the little containers off at the lab. This time I do it right, but the lab loses all the specimens. We have to do the whole test all over again.

It's recess. Actually, isn't preschool pretty much all recess? I'm outside in the yard at preschool, watching Josh play tag with two girls. He's cute, with blond hair and blue eyes, even though he's Jewish, like me. He's trying to catch the girls. I remember one of them has Mary in her name, she's a Mary Anne or Mary Beth, and she has straight hair that catches the light and takes flight in the wind, and there's the flutter of a thin ribbon, flapping with the speed of the chase. He's trying to kiss the girls and they squeal and run away. I run alongside them, past the big windows, with leaf-and-wax-paper crayon pressings taped to the insides of the windows, and I shriek like the girls do, waiting for them to look back and see me and grab my hand and pull me with them into the cover of the trees, and I giggle, wanting Josh to hear me and turn around and choose me as his next target. I want him to chase after me and catch me and kiss me.

They don't. He doesn't. I already know I'm not like them. I already know I'm not pretty and little and squealy. My hair is wavy and curly and thick. Part of what makes me different is those girls don't seem to want Josh to catch them, and I do want him to catch me. For them, there seems only to be the chase and the thrill and the joy of running with another girl. But me, I'm inside myself, observing, apart, and knowing this before I am six years old.

I stare at my hands. I've got Magic Marker and dried Elmer's glue on them, peeling off like an old sunburn. I go find the teacher and help her set up for the next art project. She gives me my pills to take three times a day. All the teachers know: my mom tells them and I remind them if they forget that they have to take me aside and give me my pill. At first they ask me if I want a cup of water, but soon they stop asking. I am proud that I take my pills without water and enjoy the admiration of adults who say, "Oh, I could never do that, I hate taking pills without water." No other kids take pills. No other kids have medic alert bracelets. I tell people that I can't take my bracelet off, even during swimming. I tell everyone about my Adrenal Hyperplasia, my enzyme imbalance, that something wasn't making enough in my body and something else made too much and I might have been short so I have to take medication to make me start puberty on time and that I might start developing early and might even get to wear a bra soon.

Developing is the word for growing breasts. Breasts are cool, but wearing a bra is even cooler. I can't wait to wear a bra. Girls who wear bras have boyfriends. I see movie stars kiss on TV, their heads twisting back and forth for a long time. I want to kiss like that someday. I look at my boobies all the time to see if they are getting larger. Every time I see my Gram I ask her if my boobs are getting larger. She says she'd need a microscope to see them. I press them together to make cleavage. I see the little freckles under my arms and on my chest and wonder if they will ever be on a booby, rather than just on regular skin, like they are now.

Telling

I pull at your nipples tentatively at first, through your tank top, not sure what hurts or what doesn't. Your surgery was a year and half ago so it might be long healed by now, but I know the place where my appendix was removed was sensitive for more than a decade.

You tell me that it doesn't hurt, but there are places that are numb. You poke around to feel the places that don't feel.

The thing about activism, about telling your story, is you don't know it's going to hurt; there's no sign, no warning.

The young college student I met last week, the one who just came out as intersex, says parts of his penis are numb. He tells women that his stamina makes up for his loss of length and sensation. He can go for a real long time.

And even though there's no sign, sometimes when someone wants me to tell my story, wants me to tell them about intersex, there's this raw aversion. It's not numbness. It's just this odd feeling, this quiet no.

My mom asks me to speak to her book group about *Middlesex*. I'm surprised that my mom asked, because everyone talks to me about *Middlesex*, and I felt I would have mentioned it to her... but I must not have, or maybe I did but she just didn't understand. Anyway, I said no. I felt guilty for saying no, but I couldn't explain why I didn't want to talk to her group. I couldn't begin to explain what it had been like when Middlesex was first published. How I had been in touch with the editor of *The New York Times* op-ed page; how, when the book came out, I spent every minute for a week trying to write the perfect op-ed about the intersex response to *Middlesex*; and how, after writing nine versions, consulting with famous writers and journalists about the piece, and submitting two to this op-ed editor, the piece didn't get published. I couldn't tell her that during that same week I heard Jeffrey Eugenides read from *Middlesex* at Books Inc.; couldn't tell her that he used the word "hermaphrodite" instead of "intersex," as if it were appropriate; that he spoke as if he were a doctor, using the phrase "5 Alpha Reductase syndrome" in place of a medical degree he doesn't have, calling on artistic license as an excuse for exoticizing his dream hermaphrodite, for being yet one more person profiting off the selling of intersex people as freaks of nature.

I couldn't tell her that after I met him I got in my car to pick up my genderqueer lover who was at a meeting for PISSR (People in Search of Safe Restrooms), and that when he sat down next to me in the car, I started crying. Crying because Eugenides, who'd never actually talked to an intersex person before he published that book, had access to so many millions of people, and that I couldn't get an op-ed published. Crying because I sat there while he read from his book and while he answered questions as if he were an expert, as if he knew about intersex, and I sat there, an expert, silent and fuming and hot with shame as he called me and people I love hermaphrodites.

I mean, I could have told my mom all this. But I chose not to. Somehow, I just couldn't muster the energy.

Three weeks later, my mom called me. She had just finished reading *Middlesex.* When I asked her what she thought, she said, "Oh my God, it was us. It was your story. It was my story. And there's no way I want to talk about it in my book group. It's too personal."

I felt my mom really understood how I felt, that it seemed impossible and too intimate to sum up our story within the space of a book group and the confines of the "intersex" label. Later, she told me she hung up the phone and started to cry, and then she started to sob. She said she cried harder than she ever had in her life, pacing around her house, unable to stop. She finally called a friend because she knew she couldn't be alone. She said to me, "In the book, the parents of the intersex person talk about it, but it wasn't that way for me, I never talked about it. I never cried about it." Thirty years later, she finally did, sensation coming back to parts of her heart that had been numb for years, tingling in a sleepy limb. There's a cost to telling our story, a cost to no longer being numb.

My hands were tentative at first, touching softly. Yours were never gentle, but they were sure. You hurt me just the right amount, waking the parts of me that are gentle, that are soft. I yielded, not telling you anything, no stories, nothing really about myself, letting my body ache, pain replacing numbness, the body a place of healing instead of the brain.

Opinion

People keep asking me about Jeffrey Eugenides' new novel *Middlesex* because the main character is considered a hermaphrodite and so am I. But really, neither of us are. Outside of myth, there are no hermaphrodites. It is physiologically impossible to be both fully male and fully female.

But you can be born with a mix or blending of male and female parts, known as "intersex," and indeed this is what Eugenides' protagonist Cal and I have in common. People with intersex conditions are those who were born with sexual anatomy that someone else decided isn't "standard" for males or females.

Unlike Hermaphroditus, the mythical creature who was both a man and a woman, people with intersex are not magical. We're not even that rare. Each year, more than 1 in every 2,000 babies are born with an intersex condition, which makes intersex more common than Cystic Fibrosis. Intersex conditions include Congenital Adrenal Hyperplasia, Klinefelter's Syndrome, Androgen Insensitivity Sydrome, and Gonadal Disgenesis, among others. Why all the mystery and secrecy then? Because we're talking about genitals, here, and sex. And our intersex bodies have become collision sites for Western society's obsession with sex and fear of difference.

Intersex bodies are considered freakish because society has fallen prey to the myth that humans are sexually dimorphic, that is: all women look like X and are designed to have sex with men, while all men look like Y, are designed to have sex with women. Problem is, that's just not what happens in real life.

In real life, variations in genes, hormones, and maternal

environments mean that some boys are born with very small penises or undescended testes, and some girls are born with enlarged clitorises or without a vagina. More and more people—including parents and doctors—are learning that our intersexed bodies are just naturally occurring variations. Unfortunately, many people in hospitals with decision-making power consider our genitals defective, even though in most cases they are perfectly healthy.

Each day in the U.S., five babies are subjected to unnecessary plastic surgery on their genitals. It's standard operating procedure to treat an intersex birth as a pychosocial emergency and to perform cosmetic sexual surgery as early as possible. There's another myth that intersex will go away with "corrective" surgery. It doesn't. But sensation often does.

Yet many people, including physicians who treat intersex, remain under the illusion that technology can and should fix everything, and that anything that's different should be corrected, regardless of risk. This belief keeps them from listening to real people with intersex conditions, many of whom challenge unnecessary surgeries. (None of us object to surgery that preserves health or life, but these surgeries are performed for psychosocial reasons, not medical ones.)

Sometimes I think they just don't want to hear the real stories. I get cynical and think, who wants the everyday details of someone's life when you can use people with intersex to fulfil erotic fantasies, narrative requirements, and research programs? People with intersex continue to be used to satisfy the interests of others: as scientific specimens, teaching models for medical students (naked, of course), literary metaphors, gags for popular sitcoms, and lastly where we at least might get a cut of the profits as circus freaks and peep show attractions.

Intersex has increasingly been in the public eye, due to the work of the intersex rights movement, led largely by the Intersex Society of North America. The result has been that Eugenides and others are now realizing how compelling the idea of intersex is. Problem is, few of them are actually talking to people with intersex. But we've been here all along and we have plenty to tell. What we have to say may shock and surprise you: We're not actually all that different.

We are women, men, and alternative genders such as transgender—just like non-intersex people. We are straight, gay, married, single—just like non-intersex people. We like to decide what happens to our bodies and like to be asked about our lives, rather than told. We've told our own stories in books, websites, newsletters, and videos. I can promise you they are far more compelling and exciting, moving and powerful than any fictionalized account. While the myth of Hermaphroditus has captured the imagination for ages, it traps real human beings in the painfully small confines of story. Someone else's story.

Care

Before my Gram went to live with my uncle in Santa Fe, where she died a few months later, she lived in the Traditions (read: Alzheimer's) Unit of a local old-age home. I arrived twice to find that Gram had no glasses. With fewer than forty residents in a locked ward, I didn't understand where her glasses were going. Then there was the time one of the other caregivers told me Gram's dentures were missing. She went to a box full of dentures and picked one out that could have been Gram's but who could tell? So she put on gloves and had Gram open wide. She tried to put it in the empty space, forcing it, but the big teeth clearly didn't fit, and she still pushed a bit harder and made Gram bleed, and I stood by and watched this.

These caregivers were the same women though, who told me Gram's pants were too tight and that she needed new ones. Neither me nor my mom or my dad had thought to buy her new pants. She'd probably had the same pants for forty years. Way before her osteoporosis made her bent over completely, almost at a right angle, facing the floor and making her middle that much wider. No, we didn't think of that.

And these were the women who told me it's cheaper to buy Depends than use the ones the unit could provide, even though that's what my dad had opted for, saying, "Who wants to buy those, right?" Well, I did. They fit more like underwear than the diaper-like other brands. I thought Gram would prefer those, the "pull-up" kind and hoped she didn't think of baby pull-ups.

All the caregivers seemed to love Gram and they all always had stories about her. Like the time she came out of her room at 2 a.m. with gold paint covering her face. She had thought it was a moisturizing mask. It took the caregivers hours to remove.

Gram was so bent over that her bras no longer fit her. One of the caregivers told me it didn't make sense to buy her new bras because she didn't really need the support anymore, plus she was wearing them on the outside of her clothes by mistake. She recommended camisoles. So I take Gram to the Blackhawk mall. Where no one in the cavernous marble-floored department store is there to help you. And while the trip probably takes a day off of Gram's life for how much it tires her out, I take her anyway, just to get her out of the unit for a change of scene.

As I'm pulling Gram into a camisole, I notice a smell. Nothing like body odor or the urine I'm so scared of smelling on her, but something worse, something rotting or unclean. And the horror of it is that I have no idea where it's coming from and one minute I smell it and the next minute I don't and God knows I don't want to find it. I get her in and out of several camisoles. The black lace causes her to remark, "What, are you getting me ready for my wedding night?"

I buy her the loosest ones that still seem to fit, where the straps stay on her shoulders, because the tight ones press her breasts ridiculously close to her chest, and her breasts, long and flat, almost poke out the bottom hem and I'm sure that's not the look Gram's after. Although I'm not so sure she's after any look, just interested in pleasing me, and frustrated because we're shopping for her and not for me. She says shopping for her is just pointless. I tell her next time we'll shop for me.

Which we were kind of doing in a way, anyway. When we moved Gram from the second place in Oakland to the Traditions Unit, we had to get rid of most of her clothes. She so badly wanted me to wear her clothing and yet none of it was anything I would ever in a million years wear. She bought most of her clothes during the era that polyester was invented and no fabric would ever replace polyester in my grandma's heart, and so there was nothing I would wear from those closets. Nothing, except the slips.

There were full-length white ones with gray lace trim, cream-colored slips with embroidered seashells, brown half-slips. It was a treasure trove of tight and slinky nightclub wear that my grandma would never in a million years approve of. I love them all and wear them often. I can't help thinking as I pay for the camisoles that they too might be mine someday.

On the way out of the store, Gram tells me she needs to pee, and I'm glad she tells me and that she still knows this. I ask her if she wants help because it's been a long time since we've had an occasion to use a bathroom together and she surprises me by saying yes. So we use the disabled bathroom and I help her stand and balance, and to my great relief she wipes herself, but then she tosses the toilet paper down her pants rather than the toilet.

The next time I visit Gram, Iris—my favorite caregiver, the one who tells me what's up, the real deal—tells me that Gram has a bad infection under her breasts and not to worry, they had a doctor check it out and now she has cream for it, and Iris had just had my Gram lay flat on the bed to apply it to the infection and now it's getting better. I ask Iris how Gram got the infection and she says from not bathing under there. What do I say? She can't bathe by herself. They bathe her. We all know this. Don't they know that you have to bathe old women under their breasts? Don't they smell what I smelled, and if they do, how does it feel to ignore it? I thank Iris for the information, grateful at least that she told me the truth. I feel terribly guilty and completely powerless.

One week before Gram left the unit for good, I rush over to visit for an hour before I'm going to drive back to Oakland to pick up my girlfriend to then drive back to San Francisco for my ex-girlfriend's wedding, which will be the first Jewish queer wedding I have ever attended. During the hour-long drive over to Danville, I consider whether to tell Gram I'm going to a gay wedding. Everywhere we ever went together—through the hallways of the unit, in a supermarket, in a restaurant—she would eye, evaluate, and then flirt with every man that we passed. For me. She was overt and completely relentless. When she wasn't flirting with strange waiters, delivery men, and grocery shoppers, she was doggedly asking me over and over, what nice young men am I dating, why can't I find myself a rich doctor or lawyer, when am I going to get married, who is going to take care of me? She was inconsolable when I told her I was gay, and now she seemed to forget it on a conveniently regular basis. I decided not to tell her the gay part of the gay wedding. Dressed in my almost sexy, a little bit revealing blue dress, I don a sweater to cover up a bit and enter the back of the Traditions Unit, noting that the doors are open, which is odd. They are usually locked and I usually key in a code to enter.

"Oh, how did you make it so soon?" the caregiver who meets me at the door asks excitedly. "You beat the paramedics!" I have no idea what she's talking about and ask her to slow down, and another caregiver rushes over to tell me that my grandmother is sick, that she threw up and lost consciousness, and that they can't revive her. I run over to the circle of chairs that surround the TV, and there she is, slumped in a chair, head lolling a bit, eyes closed, yellow-brown puke down her nightgown. I take her hand and try to talk to her. She revives a bit and then the paramedics arrive and lie her down and ask the caregivers what happened. And no one knows. The paramedics look to one caregiver and then another to tell them what happened when, how long she'd been unconscious, when she threw up, and the one caregiver who does know is so panicked that language fails her and she can't speak English, and so the paramedics look to me—the white woman, the family member, the only person holding Gram—and I have to tell them I wasn't there, I just arrived. I am scared but also beginning to get angry that these women can't tell the paramedics what they need to know to help Gram.

In a few minutes, I have met all four paramedics, and Gram is awake and talking and disoriented, but that's nothing new. It's decided that even though Gram looks fine you can't be too careful with an 89-year-old so we're going to the emergency room. As I'm on the way out to follow the ambulance to the hospital, one of the paramedics tells me he can tell I'm a good granddaughter. And as I drive to the hospital, I catch myself wondering if there's any way I can still make it to the wedding.

At the hospital, Gram is whisked into many rooms, for many tests. And then brought back. So I wait in her little emergency room.

And chat with her when she's brought back. She is awake and answers questions when asked and is feeling just fine, except a little cold and they pile warm blankets on her. Main problem is she can't really remember passing out or feeling ill. She has some vague idea that something has happened, but she's not even sure that it's her it happened to. What she is sure of is that the hospital is chock full of handsome men, doctors some of them even, and when the paramedic comes in to say they're leaving, she comments loudly to me that he is very handsome and how hard would it be to marry a handsome man like him? He smiles that isn't-she-cute smile on his way out. And I'm reminded once again that I'm supposed to be on the road, driving to pick up my girlfriend, and then going to my ex-girlfriend's wedding in the park, with all these other fabulous queers.

My parents are away, but they have been notified and call me at the hospital. I tell them what's going on, but there's really nothing they can do from up there in Oregon. And we're all sure she's fine, but the tests have to be taken, and then processed, and then analyzed before they can release her. It's Sunday morning at Danville General, where the biggest emergency besides Gram is a little girl with an upset stomach that started while she was on a cruise. As Gram is waiting for yet one of many more tests, I call my girlfriend and tell her I won't be able to make the wedding. I'm so disappointed I nearly cry and hate myself for how selfish I'm being. When I get off the phone, a guy wearing scrubs in the emergency room hands me some papers that say something about Medicare and he has me sign them and then he asks, "Can I tell you, you have beautiful eyes?" And I want to tell him, "No, you jerk," but what I say instead is, "No, that's not why we're here." (Even though my grandmother would beg to differ. But I don't tell him that either.) I go to Gram's little emergency room, but the curtain is pulled, so I go sit on the orange plastic chair outside her room.

One by one the tests come back normal. I get lunch for Gram and me from the deserted cafeteria. We split a brownie and a banana and a tuna sandwich. I have not seen her eat so much in months. And we have the same conversation for the seventh time. And in some ways, this is great, because I haven't spent more than four hours with Gram in a long time, but mostly it just sucks because spending more than two hours with her means I have to tell the same story, answer the same questions, hear the same complaints over and over until I just want to scream, so I usually end up pacing myself with little visits more often. But this endless day in the emergency room with its looped and loopy conversation is just made more painful with each male doctor, nurse, or janitor that enters the room and is then subjected to my Gram's flirting and propositions of marriage, on my behalf, of course. And don't ask me how she knows, but when an obviously gay technician comes in to take the final test of the day, she jokes with him about everything, but not once mentions to him that he, too, could be my future husband.

The final straw of the day arrives in the form of two nurses who tell me they are going to wash Gram, and they emphasize "wash" as in wash well, as in, wash well down there. It's evident to them that she hasn't been cleaned very well. Maybe for several days. And they tell me that they have heard some stories about that place where she's staying. And, because they can't do any less, and certainly no more, these two nurses wash Gram before I take her back to the Traditions Unit. By four p.m., Gram is clean and has a clean bill of health.

I take her out to the car in a wheelchair. Drive her back to the unit. All the caregivers are relieved to see her, to hear she is fine, glad to have her back.

I am too worn out to bring up what the nurses at the hospital said. I am glad they are happy to see Gram. I just want to go home.

Lessons

I think most girls in America grow up thinking they're fat. Usually this happens in the early teens, or even younger for some. For me, it started when I was six.

I was six when my Congenital Adrenal Hyperplasia was brought under control with medication. I was monitored very closely to make sure the medication was mimicking what my hormones would have been doing if they were doing the right thing on their own. In addition to my hormone levels, my weight and height were watched closely because of the relationship between androgens and sexual development.

The doctor told my mom I needed to lose weight in order to postpone the onset of puberty. This meant diets and exercise. I can still remember at what age I was sixty-six pounds, then seventy-four pounds, eighty-six, and then the horror of being over 100 pounds. 104. What a terrible number. I knew I was fat. At a family vacation with my grandparents in Palm Springs, I was embarrassed to be photographed in a bathing suit. My parents were on the Scarsdale diet, so they put me on it, too. Breakfast was a slice of bread, some melon. I would bring tuna, carrot sticks, and grapefruit to school for lunch. Everyone else's food looked better. They got to eat little bags of Fritos, cookies, and juice drinks. It was my mom's job, mostly, to help me, teaching me how to watch my weight, encouraging me to think before I ate, and taking me to a weight loss counselor in San Francisco. The weight counselor gave me a book for overweight teens. She said technically I was overweight but not obese. In truth, I never had more than a dozen pounds to lose, but they were huge pounds. The book taught fat kids how not to overeat, how to try eating thirteen cookies rather than fourteen cookies. I had never eaten that many cookies at once in my entire life.

"Are you sure you want to eat that?" and "Do you really need that?" became familiar refrains. Family and friends got in on the deal. One night after dinner in North Beach, my mom's friend offered to buy me my first pair of designer jeans if I could walk up a big steep hill and back. My grandmothers both helped me diet, buying cottage cheese and salad for my visits, not offering the usual Oreos and homemade caramel bars. There's a picture of me taken by my grandma during one of my visits to Santa Barbara. I'm roller-skating along the boardwalk, and I'm about ten years old. I remember feeling fat that day, ashamed that she was taking the picture, wondering how to stand to make my thighs look thinner. Today, if anyone else looks at that picture, including me, they'd see a happy, fit, healthy girl. That's not how I felt then, though.

The other lessons I was learning about my body at this time came from religious school. As an adult, it's become clear to me that not everyone grew up watching those movies. And if you're Jewish, you already know what I'm talking about. Year after year, we sat paralyzed in tiny, cramped wooden desks or in a circle of folding chairs, and watched them. Take second grade, for example, Marc Berg's class, which was held in a little room above the reception hall. The blinds were drawn, lights dimmed or off completely, and the only movement in the room—because none of us kids was even breathing, let alone running around—was the bleak black-and-white flickering of footage from the 1940s. We'd see families waving from the trains, people herded into camps. There were naked, gaunt figures staring from behind fences; bulldozers shoving piles of barely recognizable, unclothed, twig-like limp bodies into ditches.

And I watched, horrified, guilty, thinking, Those are my people. Those are Jewish people, just like me, from where my grandparents and great-grandparents are from. I wondered why I escaped that fate, why someone from my family escaped somehow, because here I was today watching this from far away. Why? And guilty and ashamed, too, because I was titillated. I was in grade school and these were the first naked bodies I'd seen—dead or alive—besides my family. The films were the most perverse things I'd ever seen, maybe ever have seen. These were pictures of real people, unconsenting to everything that happened, including their nakedness. They weren't supposed to be viewed. I knew this. And any pleasure, any excitement, however small, at seeing naked bodies that I wasn't supposed to be seeing welled up inside me.

After seeing the films, I was marked, the invisible yellow star emblazoned on my flushed face. And the shame and the recognition and the fascination would return to heat my face every time I saw images of Jews from World War II.

The pictures of the torture that was done to the Jews in the operating rooms, the mountains of hair, the human-skin lampshades, the gold fillings plied from Jews' teeth, even the fingernail scratches on the ceilings of the gas chambers: all these images made me aware of my body as a Jewish body. Some kids in America escape thinking of holding their breath in the gas chambers, don't have to wonder if they would have been strong enough or pretty enough to have been chosen, saved, used by the Nazi soldiers. Some kids don't have to imagine being reduced to a naked, starving vessel of pain that has seen the unimaginable, that gets liberated way too late by the Americans. They don't have to wonder why the Americans waited when they knew what was going on over there, or what their Jewish families, in America at the time, were doing while all this was going on in their homeland. And they don't have to wonder what it is about them and their families that made other people want to exterminate them.

So there I was, in second grade, thinking about stacks of naked bodies, torture, deprivation, hiding, and shame about my identity. Being Jewish gave me a sense of my body as being unsafe, or more accurately, as dangerous, as the thing that gives me away—as a Jew, and also as someone with desires that come from unspeakable places.

Invisible

I was twenty-one when I first went to an S/M club by myself. I was in New York for the first time, on a six-month field study. Like everything else I knew about sex, I had learned about the Catacombs sex club from reading books. Gay porn. John Preston, to be exact. I couldn't get enough of the scenes of hot, muscled men dominating each other, humiliating each other, fucking and sucking each other. And for some reason, I had no qualms going to a club, by myself, where this kind of thing would be going on. I asked my gay roommate if the Catacombs still existed. He told me it had closed years ago, but there was a place called the Vault. I decided it sounded hot and I wanted to see it.

I finished off my six-day week of community organizing in Crown Heights, and then spent the rest of the Saturday waiting for it to be late enough to go out. I ventured over to the Meatpacking District, and it was perfect: dark, industrial, factory loading docks all closed shut. I found a mailbox at the top of a flight of stairs that matched the address that John had given me. I wasn't ready to go down those stairs yet—it felt too early, and I felt too sober—so I wandered into a bar on the corner called Hogs and Heifers. It had been open for only three weeks. It was a small bar populated with off-duty cops, local artists, and faux rednecks. I had a beer while I screwed up the courage to go down those dark stairs. Having a beer was new for me, too—just walking in somewhere and being old enough to drink. A cute guy at the bar came on to me. He was older, and a jeweler. He introduced me to the sexy lady bartender and the owner of the place and some other patrons. I ended up going back to the bar a bunch of times, bringing all sorts of people, and becoming a regular. It was a hip, seedy New York version of *Cheers*.

When I finally felt brave enough, I walked down the dark steps to the Vault. I walked through some dark curtains, right past the guy who would ordinarily, I guess, be taking money or checking IDs. I felt invisible as I walked into what looked like a regular bar at first. I ended up getting in free the first few times I went to the Vault, and didn't find out until I brought a male friend with me that they actually charged a cover. Maybe they had a policy about letting women in free, or maybe they were scared I was bait for a sting operation.

Trying not to look too terribly naïve, I looked around the room and saw S/M equipment for the first time. It looked like what I'd read about in books, but even more intense than I'd imagined. In the brackish yellow light, I saw a huge wooden cross with eyebolts sticking out of it. There were things that looked like sawhorses, and things that looked like machines you'd see at a gym, and various other types of equipment that I didn't have the experience or the imagination to figure out, but that consisted of wooden beams, studs, leather, and a lot of metal. Across from the cross, there was a naked potbellied man strung up by his arms from chains that hung from the ceiling, his feet just barely touching the ground, being whipped by a woman so hard that huge welts rose on his back, ass, and legs.

I walked into a small room off that main area. It was dark, with a trough that ran through it, smelling of piss.

Back in the main room, I glanced down as I was walking, and there was a man, shackled in chains, covered in torn rags, shuffling on the floor around people's ankles as they drank at the bar. The floor was wet in areas and he still crawled around down there.

Looking around, I was surprised to find that the club was full of men. Not only that, but they looked like straight men. The only woman was the one whipping that man. And one time there was a fancy dressed-up woman who looked like she was probably a man, too. She flirted with the male friend I brought. At the time I probably would have called her a transvestite. Now I'd probably call her a transwoman. And probably a sex worker, too. That first night, looking around the Vault, I was shocked to realize that S/M wasn't an innately queer activity, and that it was possible for it to not look sexy at all to me. I wondered if anyone would approach me. No one did. No one said a word to me. Actually, I don't think anyone even made eye contact with me.

More than a decade later, I'm not surprised that no one ever did. I must have seemed so out of place, a fresh-faced college girl who didn't wear makeup, whose primary knowledge of fetishes was the negative definition I'd learned from my women's studies classes. I'd learned that fetishizing was the oppressive act of focusing on certain parts of women's bodies, like their breasts or their legs, to the point of reducing them to only that body part. There had been no mention of leather or S/M clubs in those classes. Those things I learned from my classmate Susan, who lent me her vibrator and books by Pat Califia and Carol Queen. I didn't even know what to wear at an S/M club, let alone how to flag my hidden desires. My idea of dressing up to look sexy was to wear my jeans (baggy, of course) and a black T-shirt (loose, of course) with a collar that had been cut off à la Flashdance. For a finishing touch, I would wear a rosary or a Mexican silver cross—a throwback from the long-gone Madonna days, yes, but also a huge rebellion for a nice Jewish girl like me. Wearing a cross or bloodred rosary beads made me feel kind of wild.

At the time, I was surprised no one talked to me. On some level, I think I expected to be welcomed into the Vault, taken on a tour of the underworld, taken by the hand and introduced politely to the illicit arts of rough sex, pain play, and submission. Truth is, I had no idea what I was looking for, and I probably flagged that ignorance more clearly than anything else. Now I know I was looking for someone to take me, take me down in particular. I wanted to lose control, but only because someone would take it from me. And not because I had explained it to them, but because they could read me, could see through me, could see what I wanted, and then could tease me and deny me what I wanted until I begged, tears streaming shamelessly down my cheeks... or something like that.

And even though nothing like that happened at the club that night,

I left feeling exhilarated. I had experienced a New York S/M club own my own, without company, without supervision, without permission. I went back to the Vault several times. It was part of an education that was just beginning, a field study about courage, desire, and having no idea where I was going, but hoping I would know it when I got there, or better yet, that someone there would recognize me.

First

During my junior year as a transfer student at UC Santa Cruz, I met Lauren. I remember the first time I saw her. I could hear her and smell her before she entered Kresge lecture hall: little bells hung from her hair wraps, adorned her wrists and ankles, perhaps warning little birdies of this fierce little cat who pranced around without shoes but with enough patchouli to choke a horse.

We were both newly bi, Lauren and I. She shaved her head weeks after I met her. I was the co-facilitator of the Bi Women for Women club on campus, a bold move seeing as I had never even kissed a woman and had no idea if I'd really like it if presented with the opportunity. I had joined the group because the flyers around campus said it was a group for bi, questioning, and non-labeling women, and I knew that I was at least the last two if not the first.

I was pretty ignorant. Up until my junior year in college, I thought there was only gay and straight. At UC San Diego I had shown up to all sorts of gay events that were attended mostly by men, and all the gay people I knew were men, and I was attracted to men, so how could I be gay? I knew so little about sexual orientation that I thought bisexual meant a person had two sex organs, like a hermaphrodite, which I can say now, but I can tell you I didn't know that word then, either.

So Lauren and I were coming out at the same time and were close friends during the adventure of it, her sleeping over once or twice in my dorm room, us talking late into the night about our bi-curiosity. We talked about getting together, maybe being each other's firsts and having sex, but she wasn't sure she'd actually like the logistics of sex with women. She told me she was particularly scared she wouldn't like pussies; she thought it might be gross. I told her I didn't want my first time with a woman to be with someone who thought pussies were slimy. We decided to just stay friends.

By the last quarter of my senior year at UC Santa Cruz, I was disappointed. Weren't these supposed to have been my wild experimentation years? Where were the all-night parties that turned into orgies? The camping trips with friends that turned naturally, lingeringly sexual in front of the campfire, under the stars? Everyone falling asleep cuddling in one bed—girls, boys, arms, legs? Where were the drug trips that facilitated all the craziness and sexuality I was looking for? I had done mushrooms, made love with a woman, come out as bisexual... but doesn't every girl do that in college? My college years were over—and with them, I thought, went all my chances to let loose and really live. I was going to move to the city—New York or San Francisco, I wasn't sure—get a job and be an adult.

Fortunately, as assumptions usually are, this one was wrong. The end of college was the beginning of the kind of life I'd always dreamed of. It all fell into place with the Queen of Heaven sex party. I'd heard about sex parties from my friend Susan, who was in my gay and lesbian lit class. Susan was my entrée into the alternative queer world. I knew what gay was. Queer was a whole different story.

"Gay" is women loving women and men loving men who want to be recognized as couples and be able to get the same rights and privileges as straight couples. Gays read *Out* magazine, cry at Gay Pride marches, watch *Queer as Folk*, and think that bisexual and transgender people are ruining everyone's chances to be perceived as normal. They believe that if we could all just act normal, we'd get good jobs, be able to get married, and earn enough money to shop at Pottery Barn. Gays wear gold.

"Queer" is men who used to be girls who love other queer girls, and boyish girls who only date other boyish girls who behave in a couple as if they are both gay men. Queer is getting off on leather or latex or polyamory, or acknowledging that there are more than two genders. Queer is understanding that gay rights are linked to all other movements for dignity and equality: women's rights, disability rights, indigenous rights, and workers' rights. Queers do not shop at The Gap; they protest The Gap. They wear platform heels, work boots, facial piercings, glitter, and tight tank tops. Queers wouldn't wear gold even if they could afford it.

So Susan was queer. She lived alone in a trailer full of books. She made me fresh tom ka gai soup, had flashing green eyes and evenly spaced silver hoops all the way up her earlobes that made me think of dragon scales. Susan lent me her books but, most importantly, let me borrow her Hitachi magic wand vibrator once when she was out of town.

I had never used a vibrator before. In fact, I don't think I'd had an orgasm before. I took her vibrator, wrapped in a plastic shopping bag, back to my dorm room. I put my Erasure tape in the stereo, thinking the electronic music would drown out any electric humming the vibrator might make. I sat on my comforter with my pants off, put a condom on the tip of the vibrator, turned on the massager, and touched it to my vulva. The sensation was immediate: tingly and tickling and better than anyone had ever touched me. Before I knew it, I was clenching and writhing and then a little bit of watery liquid came out. I saw two little puddles on my comforter. Shocked at the intensity of the feeling and my physical reaction, I turned off the vibrator. I sat there, catching my breath, giggling at the pleasure that I could just turn on and off. I felt like I'd never need a lover again. I wondered why each and every girl wasn't given a vibrator when she turned thirteen.

Trade

You want to know my secrets and lies.

You send me reminders of what I haven't told you yet.

You just left.

Here's one: The water in my bathtub runs uphill. Well, that is a lie, because it doesn't really, it just seems to because the floor tilts. It's not really a secret, just something very few people know, and thus becomes privileged information. Information that I tell you shyly because I want you to know and I'm not sure you care. It's a kind of transaction.

You begin your stories with, "Have I told you about...?" and now that you've told me so many stories, you joke that a more accurate question might be, "Do you care about...?"

I have a pain in my hand that travels up my arm to my shoulder. I've tried to figure out what it's from: driving, typing, writing? Truth is, I think I'm getting a repetitive stress injury from my vibrator. It's the only thing I do every day besides brush my teeth and walk the dog. I looked it up on one of those sheets I got at my job about how to prevent repetitive stress injuries, and one of the things that causes them is strong vibrations. And, of course, repetition. I want you to know that despite that myth about vibrators making you lose sensation over time, my clit is working just fine.

I want you to know that I have no bruises this time. I used to say the bruises always last longer. This time you're traveling back across the country, maybe to her, with my marks across your chest. Your fingers pressed too hard into my upper arms, but I didn't tell you. A kind of secret. I wanted you to feel confident. As if I could do that. As if I have that power.

Believe it or not, there are family secrets I'm not telling. All told, if told, might result in varying degrees of healing and closeness and release. But I'm learning that I don't get to decide how other people experience honesty.

We're having no contact. You and I. I decided that. It would just be too hard to long for you this much and not know if you're coming back. I said no emails. No calls. And you believed me. You took me at my word. How could you do that? Don't you know a heart can lie to save itself pain down the line?

Here's one. A secret. I hate writing. Unfortunately, it's not only what I do for a living, but also what I do for activism and performance. I don't write in a journal or even have any kind of regular writing practice. I write for release, for intimacy, for a change, for deadlines. Mostly deadlines I set for myself. To save myself some pain down the line.

Home

I'm writing to tell you I miss you terribly. Sometimes I think of coming back. Sometimes I think nothing amazing will ever happen to me again. But I thought that once before, and I was wrong that time too.

I had just graduated from college. And I was resigned to the fact that nothing interesting was ever going to happen to me again. And then I chose you, San Francisco. More specifically, Dolores Street, between the Castro and the Mission.

I remember walking by 75 Dolores and waiting a month to hear whether the person in front of me on the waiting list was going to take the best studio in San Francisco from me. I marched by the building during what must have been the second annual Dyke March. And I prayed for that apartment. The next day, the landlord offered it to me.

You were a wish come true. An eight-year adventure. Sometimes I wonder if everything that happened could have happened anywhere else. And I then, just as quickly as I wonder, I know the answer: of course not.

The decision had been between New York City and San Francisco. It had been agonizing: I had my pros and cons list—financial considerations, family proximity—but in the end, it was the pagan sex party at 848 Divisadero that made the decision for me. At the time, I was still living in Santa Cruz, where I'd graduated from college. I was nervous going to the party, and volunteered to help set up. 848 was an art space, a two-floor storefront with a dance floor and conceptual art on the walls. For the next few hours, I met tons of people who would become my friends, lovers, and community in the years to come: A curvy woman with short hair and a soft voice helped me lug mattresses up the stairs from the basement. A tall skinny boy about my age asked me to help him hang tapestries. Muscled dancer-looking boys built a low stage and risers. Two gray-haired boys with skirts and blue eyes set out gloves, latex, lube, sharps containers, condoms, paper towels, and small garbage pails. We all joked and sweat and together created a space that would make people feel like taking off their clothes. I was amazed by the diversity of the party, the strangeness of the people, and the radical acceptance of every kind of weirdness. I felt very normal for the first time. And like I'd found a place I could be myself and be accepted.

After immersing myself in that world, I found another, a world that couldn't have seemed farther away, where punk rock dykes were gathering South of Market at the Coco Club in another kind of mating ritual, one which included gathering in dive bars, drinking copious amounts of alcohol, and reading incredibly intimate poetry straight out of journals. Sisterspit made this scene fabulous, and then made it famous. The sex in this world was hidden between the crooked pen-scrawls, under stairwells, and in back alleys. I liked the alcohol and the girls, especially the ones with white tank tops and chains holding their empty wallets to their sagging pants, but I typed my poems out, and sometimes memorized them, and this kind of polish made me somehow unclear and hard to recognize.

Three blocks away another scene entirely embraced my crafted lines and careful words. The open mic at Poetry Above Paradise welcomed every kind of urban dweller—as long as we kept under the time limit. It was there that I learned to listen to poetry, really listen, to look past someone else's idea of crazy, look past someone else's idea of normal, and witness the magic that comes out of someone's mouth when the band downstairs is quiet and the poets packing the room stop gossiping because that someone just said the most beautiful, perfect line, and then did it again, and again, and devastatingly again.

Just a few blocks from there and five short blocks from my house were Muff Dive and Red and Junk, and later one block away was Rebel Girl. This is where I went after the suffocation of holiday dinners with the family, escaping the closet of not coming out because it just didn't come up in conversation. I would run to Blondie's, dance my ass off, and remember myself. There was a particularly weird night after the wedding of my closest childhood friend. One of her friends whom I'd met at the bridal shower was a wild blonde who drove a Miata with no glass in the windows and who applied mascara while driving sixty miles per hour. She must have known I was queer and decided to live out her bi-curiosity by flirting with me on the dance floor at this wedding, in front of everyone I'd known since I was a kid. The reception was at a fancy place downtown with an iridescent ceiling that looked like the inside of a shell. I kept joking that it was fabaloney. As soon as I left the reception, I headed to Red. The girl followed me there and came onto me, trying to kiss me. After a few dances, I convinced her she was too drunk to drive and hailed her a cab. As I walked home, I passed her naturally air-conditioned Miata and pictured the homeless guy who'd probably sleep in it that night. As I turned onto Dolores, I spotted two abalone shells lying on the sidewalk, still dripping with kelp and seawater.

My favorite club was Litterbox. I found many dirty girls there. One time I went looking and left after twenty minutes with a girl I'd never seen before. She took me home on her motorcycle, to her room equipped with a Saint Anthony's cross. I told her, "No hickies the night before Passover." She didn't listen of course, or it happened too fast, or it felt too good. She spanked me hard and I didn't sleep over and we never talked again, although I saw her around for years.

Later, Mecca opened a block from my house and forever stole any legal parking spaces. I was only in there one time. I went in with friends—I can barely remember who, except I think it was with this one guy that I bonded with while at a circuit party in Potrero on Pride Day. There were two people amidst the sea of dancing boys that didn't fit in: me—the girl—and him, the boy in overalls that wasn't super-fit and muscley. He was Mormon and had just moved from Utah. He took me to Mecca and introduced me to a dot-com girl who'd just cashed in a lot of stock options. She didn't look gay; she looked nervous. She was only in the U.S. for a short time because she was going to travel the world now that she didn't have to work anymore. I found myself with her in the back of one of those new-at-the-time Beetles, with this girl who didn't seem gay at all. Her name started with a K, which always seems straight to me, except she let me fuck her in the backseat and made little noises as these two boys I barely remember drove us downtown to her car, even though I lived a block away.

When I think about you, what I miss the most is walking down Valencia, or walking up Market from Dolores to Castro and seeing five people I know who know me and are glad to see me. And the thing is, today, not one of the parties, poetry readings, or clubs still exists as they were back then, except Mecca, which should never have happened in the first place, but which was a harbinger of things to come.

Sometimes I think when I left you I lost my edge: that nod, dark T-shirt, recognition, worn pants, tall boots, instant urban understanding.

Now I live in the place of my childhood, Oakland, which has a different kind of edge unknown or at least unrecognized from far away. Most of us here are unknown to each other, even from across the street, race and class between us like bulletproof glass. Oakland needs me, though, more than you do, for she is on the edge, her queerness unfolding, fresh and wet, something to shape and be shaped by.

Education

What I remember most about sixth grade is not that I got to be Fern in *Charlotte's Web* in the school play, and even got the sought-after role of the dog in *The Grinch Who Stole Christmas*. What I remember is the Sex Ed incident.

At my middle school, Sex Ed was this cool thing you got to do in sixth grade for three weeks instead of science. Mrs. Bettinger, the favorite teacher, taught it. She was cool. Her classroom was like someone's living room. There was a big Persian rug on the floor, some cozy couches, and lots of plants. During study time, sometimes she played music. In Sex Ed, you write any question about sex on a piece of paper and stick it in her anonymous question box, and she would answer it the next day in front of the class. Sometimes the questions were jokes, but she would just laugh, and then answer them.

One day, one of the questions was, "I think this girl in our class is a lesbian and that she's coming on to me. I don't like it. What should I do?" The whole room got really quiet, and everyone was looking at me, or at least it felt that way—one of those times where all eyes are on you, everyone gets out of focus besides you, and your shame pulses neon, loudly, within all the quiet stares and attention. I realized right then, through the weight of all the judgment, that everyone thought that the question was about me. Thing is, I didn't even know what a lesbian was. I just knew that whatever it was, it had to do with sex and it was bad.

Mrs. Bettinger took the question seriously and answered it, but I have no idea what she said. Those words are lost, just like they were right then, when all I could feel was a hot embarrassment and anguish, and all I could hear was the blood rushing between my ears and to my face. I remember feeling like Mrs. Bettinger, too, thought the question was about me, and that she did nothing to defend me. There was no ally for me in that classroom anywhere. I didn't know what it was about me that made people so uncomfortable, but I got the feeling that it was worse and that I was more different than I even knew.

Already

The first time we had sex, we didn't touch each other. We fucked Leah instead. I went in between the two of you, so much white cotton: boxers and tank tops and T-shirts.

Even her music was young: Grateful Dead and the Cure. How many times did we shake the bed so hard the plug came out of the wall and the music stopped?

I watched the two of you bowl, two boys, gangly and then surprisingly full or strong. I told Julie I'd pay to watch the two of you in bed together. You: light and sweet, older; and her: not old enough to hide her excitement or her pain. Julie caught you looking me up and down.

Leah bought me beer, but you bought me a dance. A small, but not so small, miracle: you were as excited as I about Dance Dance Revolution.

Me on the bottom, fingering Leah's clit as you fucked her.

The moment you hit her without asking.

Her giggling, looking at the ceiling, repeating, "I have so much to learn."

I kept saying, "I'm so lucky."

You got a Leatherman from the desk and cut a hole in her underwear to fuck her. At least you asked.

Here's the thing: I just had no idea. No idea you two were bowling for me. No idea when you pressed me between you on the dance floor at the club, our sweat cementing. No idea when we started pouring water on each other, spitting mouthfuls. No idea you would finally say, "Let's go somewhere," no idea that on the way home you would climb into the backseat and start making out with Leah, making her giggle nervously and moan at the same time. No idea your hand would find its way to me, reaching over the seat to grab my chest. "I can tell you're watching us," you said from the backseat, "the car keeps slowing down."

I did have an idea what you could do in bed. I watched the way you pushed her head to your crotch while you danced. And the way you ran your fingers through her hair and grabbed. And the way you didn't judge a boyish girl for highlighting her hair.

And so I kissed you deeply and avoided showing my desire. And so I fucked Leah again. And so I kept my underwear on. And so, when you asked if I ever get to New York, I said "No, this isn't real."

Lucky. The underside of your wrist. Sweet William on your hip. Swallows. Relief that I liked your tattoos. Nothing's worse than not liking the tattoos of a new lover. Except maybe not liking their art.

What I'm not saying: I was afraid to take my shirt off. You know, being the only girl in the room.

I was so hungry. You fed me. Leah, with her eyes brimming with awe and pleasure, bringing us peanut butter and toast at 4 a.m. You, shooting prana from my cunt to my heart. Twice. How bold to shoot for my heart so soon.

I took my shirt off. At first I wasn't sure how to read the silence. Leah was fixated and fed on them for the rest of the night. You tell me you almost passed out, having had no idea.

I talked to my hairdresser about you after we met that morning for the first time. I talked about you like we had already happened.

Leah kept turning to the wall, pretending to sleep, giving us time to fall in love. She didn't come home the next night, staying away, making herself scarce, for us.

What I'm not saying: I'm so scared I want to fuck everyone but you.

You lay on top of me and told her to fuck you up the ass. She'd never done it before, but you were too far gone. "You're going to have to take charge here," you said to me as she slid off your jeans.

What I didn't say: We're from the same world. I know exactly what you want.

"Tease her hole," I said. "Wait until her hole just pulls you in," I said.

What I didn't say: I don't know you or your body.

"Forget teasing," you said. "Just fuck me," you said. And she did, your weight pressing so hard into me, your breath in my mouth.

What I didn't say: We'd be so good together.

Danna made Leah a sex CD a week later. We all agreed she needed it.

What I'm not saying: I hold myself back from calling Leah because I still want to fuck her. The look in her eyes, a little drunk, a lot scared, and so filled with desire. I see now why people date people ten years younger.

I reeked of old and new sweat. But you wouldn't let me shower.

You let her fuck you but I didn't touch you because I knew it was different with us.

What I'm not saying: I didn't want to fuck you. I wanted to make love.

Or maybe I already loved you.

Name

There's this thing that happens a while after the breakup—maybe it happens over email, or maybe the phone. What happens doesn't sound like a big deal, but it is. They use your name. It sounds startling and foreign coming from them, a letter addressed to you, but for someone else? Your name on their tongue, something you haven't heard for months, maybe years. Because while you're together, there's the way they say your name, and then there's the way they don't say your name, because they don't have to, because they only talk that way to you, or at least you hope they only talk that way to you.

And sometimes that's true, and sometimes it's not, but at any rate, there's no need to for them to use your name to get your attention because they already have it; there's no need to differentiate you from everyone else in the world, because you're already different, you're the one on their hands, the nearest taste that's not theirs, the body they may know better than their own; there's no need to punctuate a conversation, mark a beginning or end, because that kind of intimacy is one continuous conversation, with pauses here and there for work, going to the bathroom, walking the dog, dinner with a friend, and sleep. You wake up and they're there; if not next to you, then near you, in your thoughts, your heart, close, and picking up the phone is the same as taking the next breath.

And so when they use your name again, you know someone else has entered the conversation; you are not automatically the second person, the you to their I. And there's a clarity, a break, as clear as a period, as clear as the spaces between the end of one sentence and the beginning of the next, that might not have been so noticeable when you were finishing each other's sentences, or not listening at all.

Ordinary

I take feeling bad personally.

There are so many things I want to tell you. I have a list. The same lists I had when we were together. Stairway walks, recipes, movies, and poems. Little lists, same as the one I have now except those lists got done and this one won't.

I want to tell you about Sam. I want to tell you how she almost saved my life. That just hours after you had called and broken up with me, there I was at that club, drinking double shots of tequila. And how typical and tragic that more than one dyke actually found my double-fisting attractive. And that then there she was, Sam, telling me she knew me from somewhere, telling me she'd been hearing about me for years, telling me I was beautiful. She followed me around like a puppy all that night. She came on so strong, I told her if she wanted to go home with me, she better back off. And she did. Back off, I mean. And she did come home with me. I barely told her anything about you, but she could feel it emanating from me like a toxic sunburn, and she held it.

And I want to tell you about last night. I felt like such a woman last night. Why is it that misery has me feeling more female than ever? Maybe it's the mascara shadows, the lack of sleep, the tequila. Maybe it's being so far outside myself, getting fucked by strange girls and seeing myself the way the way some new girl does. I look at myself and feel desirable. Funny what a breakup can do for you. Funny what being so deep in love with you can do for me. I put on my red slip last night and the slutty white mules you love so much and danced in front of the mirror. I was so satisfied with myself last night. Everything looked so good and so right, and it was okay to be beautiful and sad.

And last night was so crazy. There was me, Victoria, my brother, his girlfriend, and a stripper from Texas, all going together to the queerest event in town, the drag king show at the King Street Garage.

And last night, I could almost have fun. There were all the girls with mustaches and all the femmes dressed so high they could've been drag queens. Last night gave me hope. I could almost enjoy it, except for the all those girls kissing each other. I could handle everything except the girls making out. Why do they have to do it in public like that?

And Nic was there. Nic, who's been way more broken-hearted than me. All my exes, Nic and Kim and Zed, each of them has now broken up with a new girl and each has shown me how ordinary extreme pain and self-pity are. Sorrow is humbling. I want my pain to be fabulous. I don't need my pain to be worse than anyone else's, I just want it to be strangely, uniquely mine—art to someone else's breakdown.

And so I almost felt good last night. And then there was Sam, in her mustard—or would that be ochre—shirt and skinny tie, and she grabbed me and kissed me and squeezed hard, her arms around me from behind. And I was careful not to touch her too sweetly or kiss her at all because there were two other girls at the show that she was dating and she wanted to be single this weekend she said. Which would have been fine if she hadn't kissed me and run her hands down my hips and told me about the party after the show. Which would have been fine if then, when the dancing started, she didn't get hot and heavy with this girl I'd seen around town, whose shoes I had loved and then hunted down and who had gray eyes that glinted, dangerous and enchanting. Sam danced with the girl, right next to me, twirling her and then bringing her close against her body the way I already, after only two weeks, knew she did. And I started feeling sick and like a voyeur and moved away on the dance floor.

And so we went to leave, Victoria and I. And I felt so stupid for giving a shit about Sam when I really didn't, and for letting myself hurt any more than I already was—and then there she was. She asked, "Where are you going?" She asked, "Are you mad at me?" She said, "I'm not dating her. She kissed me." She said, "Come to the party with me." She said, "You look so pretty," which didn't help, but I wanted everything to feel good so I said yes. And Victoria said, "Make sure you have fun."

And it all would have been fine except all the girls Sam had ever dated and happened to be dating were at the party. And your best friend Ryan's housemate Carolyn was at the party, which made me panic thinking Ryan would be there and that then he'd tell you I was there with Sam, holding hands, looking like a couple at 2 a.m.—or actually maybe I was wishing he would tell you because he never would do that to you. Just like he didn't tell me he knew you were going to break up with me.

And the party would have been fun except on our way to get away from the girl in the basement that Sam was dating we went through the kitchen and ran right into the girl with the gray eyes from the dance floor. And the girl strikes up a conversation with me, and we compliment each other's hair, dresses, shoes. Sam is clearly dying next to me, obviously hot for or awkwardly having dated this girl, but I didn't start the conversation and I'll be damned if I can't play along. So then Sam says, "Can we talk?"

And she takes me outside. And she says, "I wanted to be single this weekend and here it is two nights in a row that we've seen each other." She says, "I didn't want to leave your house this morning." She says, "I want to slow down." She says, "You could get back together with your girlfriend."

Knowing you, I tell her, trying not to cry, that just isn't going to happen. I tell her it's over with you, trying not to sound too heartbroken because this discussion is about her and me, not me and you. I tell her it's a little too late to decide she wanted to come to the party alone. I tell her I'm leaving. We're at 24th and Bryant at 3 a.m., and I start to walk home because Sam doesn't have a car. She makes dildos for a living—social service work, to quote her—and there's not a cab for miles, and as I start to walk, a car slows down, and a man leans out and honks at me. Clearly, it's not safe to walk home. And fuck Sam for putting me in this situation. I recognize two of her friends leaving the party, getting into a truck nearby, and so I march back over to Sam and tell her to ask her friends to drive me home. Knowing they can't say no, I'm already on my way over to the truck, and I hop into the back and fold myself up behind the two front seats of the cab. The women are nice and don't ask any questions and take me home.

Breaking up is so ordinary. There is nothing dramatic about breaking up. I am not special. The best thing about breaking up with you is that it has nothing to do with me.

Pedicure

It's Thanksgiving Day. My mom, dad, brother, and I are at my Uncle Buddy's and Aunt Linda's place in Florida. We're drinking mojitos: vodka, tonic, crushed ice, sugar, and tons of fresh mint. If you can't act cold and cool at a party, at least you can feel it. I paint my toes out by the pool, and Mom asks me to do hers, and while I do we talk to Uncle Buddy. Who signs me up to do his toes next. He tells me that Adam, his oldest son, who's about thirty-three, got really excited to have his toes manicured recently. Buddy tells us that Adam has been getting his toes done on a regular basis. I wonder to myself if Adam is into drag, and then my uncle says that Adam is really into Halloween and I ask what he dressed up for this year, and Buddy answers, "A woman." I smile to myself, bull's-eye. Buddy then says that he couldn't ever do drag, even by himself, in his room with no one watching.

I paint Buddy's toes. Buddy is my mom's older brother. He's a little over sixty, with those things that go along with that, like less hair, more weight. The thing about Buddy, though, is that he has the gleeful, limitless, teenage-boy energy of a person who's been waiting his whole life to be a kid, who's finally allowed to play. As I'm painting Buddy's toes, my mom and I keep exchanging glances because we're shocked he's letting me, but even more amazed at how good his toes look! And he starts to see it, how good his feet look, and he says his look better than my mom's and he's going to wear sandals to our Thanksgiving dinner to see how the rest of the family reacts. He chooses a pair of black Tevas that set off his pale feet and purple nails.

The older ladies—the "sisters," my dad calls them, though none of them are related to each other—arrive in a riotous explosion of tasteful pastels. Some of them I know well—Mom's Great Aunt Alice, Mom's Aunt Lil—and there are others that I barely know or don't know at all: Linda's mom, her friend, and another lady. They move through the house to the outside patio in a group, a loud pack of crotchety crows, pecking at each other, cawing about Bloomingdale's, cooing about weddings and great-grandkids, and where to get a good deal on honey-baked ham. They see Buddy's toes. Or actually, one of them does. She doesn't say anything to him, but rather makes the rounds with the other women: "Did you see..."

Later, the subject of the toes comes up, and I realize I'm nervous about what they're all going to say. I'm starting to feel the tiniest bit cornered, but I'm not sure why. When Aunt Linda points the toes out to her friend Amy, she shrieks, "Fag!" and Aunt Linda's eighty-year-old mom says, "I'm his mother-in-law! I'm crying," and then Amy says, "Disgusting," and Aunt Linda says, "I'm glad he's in touch with his feminine side," and Amy says, "I prefer a man without a feminine side."

I realize that I have inadvertently set myself up. The painted toes are this inadvertent vehicle to bring up the guests' latent homophobia. By painting Buddy's toes, I have allowed them to safely unmask or reveal their true feelings about gay people. And then I realize that they must not know I'm queer or not see how this relates to me. Buddy laughs it all off, but I'm feeling shaken. It itches, the discomfort, just below the surface, because no one makes the connection but me. I wonder if I should come out to them, and I wonder what the point would be, and if it would just make things even more difficult and awkward for me. My close family members know I'm queer, but they don't realize the effect the comments are having on me.

I pull my mom aside to explain to her how homophobic people's responses are. As a test, she takes her Aunt Lil, her favorite aunt, to see Buddy's toes. Aunt Lil snorts and says, "He's a fifi!"

"But you don't care, do you?" my mom asks.

"No," replies Aunt Lil. "Anyone can do anything they want and it's all right by me. As long as I love you and you love me that's all that matters."

The next day, Buddy's three sons arrive to spend the rest of the weekend together. We go out on Buddy's boat, and I look to his feet to see if he has the nail polish on. He tells me he cleaned it up before they arrived.

Hard

It's Halloween, and I'm in boy drag, which means jeans, black boots (lowest heel possible, I'm sure), tight white tank top, no bra, hair slicked back. I'm packing a dick underneath my Calvin Klein boxers, and I've got smudges on my cheeks and under my eyes—anything to give me the hard-lived, I've-been-around-the-block-too-many-times look, which is kind of a tough look for me to achieve, being in my mid-twenties, with my innocent looks and pink cheeks.

I remember the feeling that night. Way too many straight couples squished into way too small a space. It's a club I've loved in the past, replete with a boot camp area, school-years bathroom with child-sized toilets, gyno/doctor exam table, cub scout setup, cyclone fencing, and glory holes, and all of it is twisty and dark and leathered. I love this space, but now it's teeming with boring male-female couples, with women sprawled out on every available inch of floor, men looming above them, pounding away. The couple I'll never forget is squished into a small corner of a doorway with so little space that with each thoughtless thrust, the woman's head bangs into the doorframe—bam, bam, bam. It turns my stomach. The friend whom I had come to the party with is involved in a heavy S/M scene that she and her girlfriend have been planning for weeks. People are watching three deep. I feel separate and far from everything. I decide to leave.

On the way out, I say goodbye to a couple of friends. They're talking to a woman who introduces herself to me as Kat, and it's perfect because she's kind of purring at me and smiling. She asks me if I'd like to play and I say no, I was just leaving, but I'll kiss her goodbye. The kiss is soft. So soft, in fact, that it makes me hard. And when I tell my friends this story, I tell them she isn't my type, and they know my type, and she definitely isn't it. She has long brown hair, purple silk lingerie, and inch-long purple nails. And when I tell this story, I talk like I've just scored, and my friends laugh, because I sound like a dude.

Which I am. I take her into a back room with a big bed, which miraculously happens to be empty. There may be a wet spot or two on the bed, but I don't care. I tell her my clothes aren't coming off. I've been with enough butches to know that this behavior will be accepted. I climb on top of her. I rub my cock against her, hard. I pull up her lingerie, pull down her silk panties, and slide my condomed cock into her. I fuck her, she comes, but she's hungry still, I can tell, so I start in with my fingers.

"I'm not sure," she says, as I push more and more fingers inside her. She thinks I'm trying to fist her, and she's right. "It's been a while," she says, and this makes me even more sure that I'm going to fist her. I feel very powerful: her, naked below me, and me, focused entirely on her pleasure, me getting off on her wetness, her shrieks, and then her writhing around on my hand, taking it in easily, like it had been yesterday, like we actually knew each other. She's a big woman, larger than me, and I sit between her legs, feeling the whole of her shake and tremor, hugely beautiful and shimmering around my small male energy. After she comes, I move up to kiss her, and then lose myself in her large breasts, surprising myself because, not having sensitive breasts myself, I often have no idea what to do with my lover's breasts. The nipple I understand, but not the fleshy part. Kat's breasts, though, I commune with. I softly run my cheek along her left breast, let the weight of it fall against my face, working with its swell and gravity, her breast the active participant and my cheeks and lips receiving. She comes again. It's only then that I notice people are watching. A couple of butches give me high fives with their eyes. I hold Kat for a few minutes, and then I leave the party, walking home along the dark, quiet streets and under the freeway, feeling untouchable, a man walking home after scoring with some chick.

I see Kat a few months later at an event I'm performing at. She smiles at me, a secret, wide-eyed, you-fucked-me-so-right smile. An I'd-do-it-again-in-a-heartbeat smile. A smile that makes me hard, and makes me leave her wanting.

Parenthood

I'm visiting my dad soon after Halloween. My mom is in Nepal, so it's just Dad and me, the wrestling on the TV turned down so we can hear each other talk. We've just gone out for Chinese food. Dad doesn't cook when Mom's out of town. He's at the mercy of family friends, who cook him dinner, and me, the excuse to go out to dinner. Sitting down in the living room, he asks me, "Who are you hanging out with these days? I feel like I have no idea what your life is like."

I can't believe my dad is asking me a question like this. It's so... sensitive. And astute. I haven't been telling my parents what I've been up to because I've been dating a ton and going to sex parties. When Dad found out I went to Gay Pride, his only response was, "I don't know how you're going to get married if you keep going to all these gay events." Dad's always been a little clueless—intentionally or not, I've never been sure. But this question is so disarming that I actually consider answering him truthfully.

"Do you really want to know?"

He says yes. So I sit him down in the living room. And I sit down across from him. It's like any sex talk between a parent and a kid, except I'm the one talking, and we're both adults, and this time it's the dad that's getting the new information. I tell him about the parties. About the talented artists I've met, the wild pagans, the performers, the lawyers. This is strategic because my dad's a lawyer. Mostly, though, I tell him about the friends I'm making, all the wonderful, creative, passionate people.

Dad listens, nodding his head, not talking, his hands at his sides. This is a big deal. My dad talks a lot, loudly, knocking into people with his large, sweeping gestures as he goes on about his current fad: marathons, boating, or 200-mile bike rides called double centuries. When I'm done with my story, he tells me, "There was a time in my life when I was very lonely, when I felt no one understood me. I know how important it is to have people around that know you."

I'm completely floored by Dad's response. I feel closer to him than I ever have before. And known in a way that's deeply comforting.

Push

I've only posed nude once. And it wasn't posing so much as an action shot. Or action shots, really. It was for a coffee table picture book with portraits of twelve women masturbating. It's called *I Am My Lover*, a remake of a popular '70s classic. It's the kind of thing you can find at stores like Good Vibrations, and that hopefully you won't find at the local porn shop. The pictures are unadorned, lit with natural light, and very intimate. I was probably about twenty-four when the pictures were taken. The photographer was my friend, Victoria, who I met at the first sex party I went to. She wrote me after and asked if she could photograph me for the book. I'd never been photographed naked before (or since), but I believed in the project. The goal was to show real women, real women's bodies, and what real women do to give themselves pleasure. Ever since Pee-wee Herman was arrested and I did a paper about society's fear of masturbation (it subverts capitalism because it so completely resists commodification), I'd prided myself on being a masturbation activist.

Even so, I was very scared to see the pictures of myself. Somehow I'd missed all those women's studies classes where you look at your vagina in the mirror and check out your cervix. I thought my pussy would look monstrous. Despite all my feminist education, I still thought the hair, the shape, the shadows would be ugly. But when I do see the pictures, I'm caught completely by surprise. My pussy, I say to myself, is gorgeous. Not new-age, sea-creature, we-moon, goddess gorgeous, but simply beautiful. And all of a sudden, I want to show the book to everyone I know. Including my mother. She's the one who taught me about the ERA and keeping your last name, she's the one who had the fish without a bicycle T-shirt. I thought surely she'd see this for the feminist act that it was.

It didn't quite go that way. I ask her if she wants to see it. She laughs, one of those laughs that comes out like a gasp of surprise, but she says yes. A week later, when I'm visiting her in Oakland, I give her the book. I tell her she can only see it if she promises to tell me what she thinks. Every time I go to visit, I see the book on her shelf, right there next to *Joy Luck Club, All the Pretty Horses*, and the studio photograph of my mom and Buddy, taken when they were kids. The book sits there for a long time. I ask Mom about it once or twice, and she always replies that she'll get to it soon. I start to wonder why she's keeping it if she doesn't want to look at it. And I start feeling like maybe it's shameful, both what I did and also showing it to my mom. But another voice says, Be proud.

A few months later, I just can't stand seeing the book collecting dust anymore. "Mom, I want the book back, okay?"

"No," she says, "I promise. I'll look at it. And I'll tell you when I have."

"Are you sure?" I ask. "You don't have to."

More time goes by and she finally does look at it. She tells me this, almost as an afterthought, when we're driving to pick up groceries. Almost all our biggest talks happen in her car, her driving, me feeling like a kid next to her in the passenger seat.

"So I looked at the book," she says. "You're so brave. You have more guts than I'll ever have. But I raised you that way, so it's no surprise."

She says this quietly. Both hands on the wheel, eyes on the road. There's no disapproval in her voice or even judgment. She sounds impressed, and also small.

"You always push me," she continues. "That's your role, you know, to push me. You always have."

I stay quiet, realizing how hungry I've been to hear what she's saying. And also scared. When I was little, she used to tell me I was pushy. This time, though, she says quite the opposite.

"You're always pushing me. And I appreciate it." My feet are folded up under me and I feel my breath catch, tight in my chest. I've waited years to hear her say that, convinced that my strength and my assertiveness were burdens to her, annoying and troublesome.

"You don't mind?" I ask her, double-checking.

"I mind," she says, "but it's good."

Another

I asked my friend Robert about the connection between testosterone and queerness. Robert is the one who invited me to my first sex party, and our friendship is one of the reasons I moved to San Francisco. I can talk to him about anything.

I wanted to talk to him because a girlfriend gave me an article about girls with CAH who desire other women because they were "othered" hormonally in a masculine direction in utero and now seek the exotic other (women) rather than men. I've heard some doctors say women with CAH have higher testosterone levels and that's why they're more likely to be gay. I wonder what is it about testosterone—on the brain, coursing through veins—that makes everyone, anyone, male or female, want to fuck women? According to medical literature and popular culture, if men want to fuck women, it's because of testosterone. And if women want to fuck women, it's because of testosterone. But testosterone isn't a male hormone; it's just a hormone. I understand that it makes people hornier, but I would think it makes them hornier for whatever they like, not that it dictates what they like. I begin to wonder what makes me queer.

I tell Robert, maybe it's because I've been othered. I tell him about having so few friends when I was little. Robert says anyone who's comfortable with sex is queer. Kids in school told me I was queer before I even knew what it was. Years later at my first Dyke March, Tasha, from my old neighborhood, said, "The kids in school told me you were gay," and I knew then that it wasn't all in my head and that sixth grade truly had been as horrible as I remembered.

As Robert and I discuss queerness, he takes his morphine and we discuss splitting pills. I show him my .25 mg of dexamethasone, and he says, "Gosh, you do weird things to your body. Why are you taking that?" And I try to explain that it stops my adrenal gland from making 17 hydroxy—or is it 21 hydroxy progesterone?—I stumble here—from making the precursor to testosterone. And he says, "Why are you doing that after the conversation we just had?"

And I realize, as I often do, that I don't know why I take my medication. I get my period on a regular basis. I might get more hair growth or acne without the medication, but I'm not even sure that would happen. I tell people the medication helps me to normalize my levels. I don't know what that means. What am I trying to become? A normal what?

Change

The first time I ever heard the word "intersex," it was from my friend Victoria, who was taking a training to be a telephone counselor for a sex information hotline. She told me there was such a thing as intersex, people born with ambiguous genitalia, and that these babies were given plastic surgery to make them look normal. She heard this from a speaker who was intersex, who had escaped surgery due to childhood illness and the fact that doctors didn't know if she'd survive surgery with her delicate health. I am blown away to hear that doctors perform surgery on babies just to make them look normal.

The next time I hear about intersex is when I meet my neighbor across the street, David. I'm walking by his house one day, and out of the blue he says, "Hey, I like your purple hair." And I say, "Hey, I like your hermaphrodites with attitude T-shirt." "Do you know about intersex?" he asks me. I tell him not really but that I saw there was film about it in the gay film festival.

"I have Klinefelter's Syndrome," David tells me. "My chromosomes are XXY, but I didn't know about my condition until my thirties. It's also why I'm so tall. My body doesn't make enough testosterone." I'm a bit overwhelmed with all the personal information, maybe even a bit embarrassed. He's not ashamed at all, unabashedly sharing information that many people wouldn't mention even if they weren't intersex, and especially to a neighbor. But David seems like a really nice guy, and I love knowing my neighbors, especially in a city like San Francisco, which is so full of apartment buildings and transient newly graduated college kids and artists who never talk to each other.

My conversation with David haunts me. I wonder if I have

something to tell him. I wonder if what I know about myself would be relevant to him; namely, that if my condition had been worse, I could have been a hermaphrodite. My mom told me that once. I remember asking her, "Why were you so worried when I was little, when I was getting diagnosed with Congenital Adrenal Hyperplasia?" She told me they were afraid I'd be a hermaphrodite.

Even after this conversation with David, I didn't really think again about intersex. Not in any major way. Until I got a call from my mom.

It was soon after Mom got back from one of her trips to Nepal. She told me she met a Nepali woman in prison whose child had ambiguous genitalia. No one over there was sure what to do with the kid, whether to raise it as a boy or a girl. Mom mentions this to me, saying she thinks the child might have CAH, the same condition that I have. She has the child's medical records and wants to find a doctor to show them to for advice. I urge my mom to hold on and not tell the people in Nepal anything or show the records to a doctor until I do some research. I quickly get off the phone and search the Internet for the word intersex. The first thing that grabs my eye is the Intersex Society of North America (ISNA). Maybe Victoria had mentioned it. I go to the website, and what comes up is a chart detailing both the current model of treatment and a more patient-centered approach to caring for people with intersex. One of the differences between the approaches is that the current approach advises surgery—early surgery, while the kid is still a baby. The Intersex Society's approach suggests assigning the child a gender and refraining from surgery unless it's medically necessary to protect the health of the child. I send my mom the URL and call her, imploring her that whatever she does, she should find a doctor who won't suggest surgery.

My mom surprises me by simply writing directly to ISNA. In her email, she writes that she knows about CAH because her daughter had it, and was wondering if this child in Nepal might have the same condition, and what course of action should be taken. The director, Cheryl Chase, writes back herself and agrees to look at the records. And then Cheryl sends an email to me.

She introduces herself, saying that my mom had mentioned my

condition and the fact that I was a poet and an activist. She says that if I am an activist, maybe I would like to go with ISNA to a queer activist conference called Creating Change, which would take place in Atlanta in two months.

I don't know what to say. It seems like Cheryl thinks I'm intersex. And while I'm honored that she includes me, I write back, thanking her, telling her that I am not intersex. All these years later, writing this, I am aware of the unintended irony: that I am so happy to be included in any group that even being welcomed by the hermaphrodites is exciting. But at the time, I feel I have to decline membership in this club. While I know CAH is an intersex condition, I have normal-looking genitals; I menstruate; I could probably have a baby even though I haven't tested this out yet, by mistake or on purpose; and, most importantly, I never had or "needed" genital surgery. Cheryl writes back that you don't have to be intersex to help fight against unnecessary surgery on intersex infants. This is compelling, unarguable logic.

After meeting David, and hearing from Cheryl, I can't stop thinking about intersex. Cheryl continues to email me and send articles, and I feel myself getting pulled toward ISNA. I tell myself that working against oppression of intersex people is really quite radical in that it's about breaking down binaries of male and female. For if we broke that down, couldn't everything fall—every assumption, every system, every simplistic formula that didn't really fit real life? Here is a seemingly tailor-made issue for me: it's about sex, it's about breaking down boundaries, and it's cutting edge—because who else do I know working on this issue?

I decide to go to Atlanta for Creating Change. All the scholarship funds are used up, so I will have to pay for my own airfare, registration, and hotel room. I decide to go anyway.

The next time I see David, I tell him I have Congenital Adrenal Hyperplasia. He nods and tells me he considers me intersex. He lends me two documentaries about intersex. One is called *Is It a Boy or a Girl?*, and the other is *XXXY*. A short documentary, *XXXY* is about two intersex people telling their stories. It cuts to the bone, with stories of childhoods full of surgery and early adulthoods filled with shame and suicide attempts. The people who tell their stories seem like anyone I might know in San Francisco. And the stories break my heart.

The second film does something very different to me. It's a Discovery Channel program that focuses on the story of one family and the birth of their child who has ambiguous genitalia due to CAH. Every time I hear the words congenital adrenal hyperplasia, I feel my face go hot. I feel like they are talking about me. And I feel shame. When the film is over, I lie on my bed, not sure what I have to feel upset about, but feeling upset all the same.

I start looking for intersex events. I go to Transgender Task Force meetings with David, where intersex is considered a subcategory of transgender. He is trying to get that changed so that intersex will be a category all by itself. At the task force meeting, they ask who is planning to attend Creating Change. I am one of two people. I am asked to help present a workshop at the conference about the task force. I agree, even though I am not even a member of the task force and have just been to a few meetings. I swap numbers with the other presenter.

Before the conference, I attempt to attend an intersex support group. The facilitator and I are the only two people who show up. When I tell Sandy, the facilitator, that I have Congenital Adrenal Hyperplasia, she seems convinced I am intersex. Those three words are like a password into a secret club. She calls my condition by its initials, CAH, like she's superfamiliar with it and says it all the time. It's as if CAH is how intersex people say it and Congenital Adrenal Hyperplasia is for people who think it's an enzyme imbalance. I join a Yahoo! group of intersex people. And I go to a screening of a film at the San Francisco Human Rights Commission with David and another intersex guy named Fred.

After the film, David, Fred, and I go for tea at the Chinese Food and Donuts corner store, the only place around that isn't already closed for the night. Not only does Fred think I am intersex, but he thinks I am transgender as well. "By taking hormones," he tells me, "you transitioned away from being intersex toward something else, toward a more traditional female." This sends my mind reeling. I wasn't sure I was even intersex, and here is someone who thinks I am intersex and transgender?

On the walk home, after Fred leaves, I ask David more about his condition and how we knew he was intersex. He tells me about his testicles not descending and being given testosterone by the doctors to make him more male. They had given him so much that it made him sick. He tells me he would've been fine being what he was, ambiguous and healthy, if only he'd had the choice. Now he is facing prostate surgery due to the overmedicating he's suffered.

I tell him, thinking out loud, that my genitals are normal and that I have a slight, borderline case of Congenital Adrenal Hyperplasia. If I were to call myself intersex at all, I think I'd say I have an intersex brain. My rationale is that those excess androgenizing hormones my body produced while I was in utero probably have affected my brain. That's also probably why I was precocious as a kid and aware of sex at an early age. And why, even now, I feel there are ways in which I am quite masculine—from being muscular to being promiscuous. David just listens and accepts everything I say. And hugs me.

I ask Cheryl if there is any help she needs getting ready for the Creating Change conference. She asks if I would help getting the T-shirts designed. I get the ad agency where I work to donate time to the project and work with a designer there to create a T-shirt. In order to do this, I have to tell my boss about intersex. And also that I think I probably am intersex. I try to say as little as possible, counting on his discomfort with a word like intersex to keep me from having to explain more. I have the shirts shipped to Atlanta. Next Cheryl asks if I could help with the banners. This is a bigger ordeal, since I am unfamiliar with banner artwork and printing and have a hard time translating the design from paper to final product. I carry the two banners with me to the conference.

For the most part, even though I am sure about the decision to attend the conference, I am pretty nervous to meet the intersex people. I don't know what ambiguous genitalia look like. I'm not sure if all intersex people look different, even with their clothes on. I wonder what people will say when they find out how little I am intersex, that my genitals appear normal, and that I've never had surgery. I wonder what other people at the conference will say about my genitals. I wonder if I will see anyone else's genitals. Despite my worrying, I'm enjoying the preconference nervousness, having been to enough retreats and conferences to look forward to that accelerated acquaintance process that always occurs, knowing that by the end of the weekend, I may be best friends with everyone from ISNA, fall in love with someone, or discover something life-changing about myself.

It doesn't quite happen that way. I arrive in Atlanta and go to the hotel where everyone is staying. And go to find the room I am sharing with Sandy, the woman who's in charge of the failed support group. I meet up with her after some time, and then she finds three others, Harlan, Katy, and Lynnell.

Once we are all in the lobby together, I ask if there is some plan for everyone to meet up together, and the only plan they know is to meet later that night at the conference center for a brief meeting. There is no plan to eat. We are in the middle of downtown Atlanta, it's after 5 p.m., and everything looks closed. We have no idea where to find cheap or healthy food. We ask the front desk about restaurants and end up at a Chinese place a few blocks away.

After dinner, we walk back to the hotel where Cheryl and her partner Robin are hanging out in the lobby with two other people I don't know yet. This is my first time meeting Cheryl in person. She is much quieter than I expected, and more shy. As a group, we walk over to the convention center. We sit in a circle on the carpet, in the corner of an upstairs landing. This is the whole group, ten of us. We go around and introduce ourselves. There is Harlan, the EPA lawyer in his mid-thirties; Katy, a tiny woman from Michigan; Lynnell, the only African American person in the group, from Chicago; Ana, another woman of color from a different part of Chicago; Natalie from San Francisco; and Sam and Mark from Atlanta. I wonder how each of these people is intersex, what surgeries they've had, what their conditions are, and if it's okay to ask.

Cheryl passes out the T-shirts. I am surprised at how appreciative people are. They can't get over how cool the T-shirts are. Cheryl and Robin outline the next two days, telling us about meetings that we'll have every morning, when our tabling shifts are, and when the

ISNA presentations are. I am waiting for some icebreaker or some introduction game. Nothing like that happens. So I just smile a lot, and my nervousness continues. I figure they must all know each other and I am the new one. But why is everyone so quiet and awkward, then?

We go to bed early. I have a hard time falling asleep. I am particularly nervous because I have my talk to give with my co-presenter, Carlos, about the San Francisco Transgender Task Force the next morning. As it turns out, Carlos is also one of the organizers of the conference. Before leaving town, I had tried multiple times to get in touch with him to plan our presentation. He was impossible to connect with. I figured he must have had it planned already, being officially on the task force and being a conference organizer. I figured his lack of preplanning was confidence that he could wing it or evidence that I wasn't going to play a large part in the presentation, which was fine with me.

I show up fifteen minutes before our talk is scheduled to begin. I'm thinking he might at least want to catch me up on what he has planned. I had hoped some people from ISNA would come to my talk to cheer me on, but no one shows up. I wait and wait. People file into the room, but none of them is Carlos. Finally, after ten minutes of stalling and telling people he'll be there any second, I decide the show must go on.

Having only been to three task force meetings, there isn't much I can tell people. I explain my predicament, tell people what I know about the task force, and then proceed to not be able to answer any of their questions about civil rights task forces, resolutions, or antidiscrimination ordinances. Finally, someone asks why I had been interested in the task force in the first place. I tell the group of twenty or so people that I am intersex and that in San Francisco, for civil rights purposes, intersex appears under the umbrella category of transgender. I explain that intersex is about sex, not gender, so it should have a category all its own. I can't quite explain why this is the case, or how an intersex person's civil rights issues are different from a transgender person's. But that doesn't seem to matter.

I am shocked to learn that most of the participants don't know about intersex. Or if they do, they don't know as much as I do. And they are hungry for information. They ask me question after question, and the majority of participants stay the whole hour and fifteen minutes the workshop had been scheduled. Many of them thank me afterward. I run into Carlos later. He had simply been caught up in meetings and missed the presentation. He apologizes profusely. And thanks me for leading the whole thing by myself.

After my workshop, I attend several other workshops, including the ISNA presentation "Intersex as a Human Rights Issue." It's presented by Cheryl Chase, the founder of ISNA, and another board member of the organization. It's an Intersex 101, so I know most of what's presented. I'm there for solidarity and to show that there's a bunch of us at the conference (we're all wearing our T-shirts). Cheryl starts off the presentation by stating that people with intersex are people whose genitals make them subject to medical intervention. I don't retain much of what's said after that because I'm stuck. I have normal-looking genitals. They might have looked strange when, at four years old, they sprouted pubic hair, but now, there's no way to tell by looking at me, even unclothed, that I'm intersex. Does this mean I'm not intersex? Should I not even be at this conference? I've had more than one doctor see me as an adult and remark at how well my treatment has gone and that I seem to have escaped looking like what other girls with CAH look like. They mention acne, hirsutism, more masculine body types. Whatever other girls with CAH look like, I don't look like it to doctors and they think I'm lucky. Now, listening to Cheryl speak, I wonder if she thinks I'm intersex. I wonder if it doesn't matter to her whether I'm intersex, just as long as I'm doing the work. I'm not even sure it matters to me in the long run; I just don't want to be caught in a lie either way. I don't say anything, and muddle through the rest of the day of workshops and speakers.

After the conference ends for the day, the ISNA crew meets for a recap. While we're waiting for everyone to show up, there's a quiet moment and I take Cheryl aside. "I hate to bug you about this, Cheryl," I start. "But your definition, that intersex is people whose genitals make them subject to surgeries or medical intervention, well, that definition doesn't include me."

I wait for Cheryl's trademark calm answer to my always well-meaning but often painfully uninformed questions. But this time it's different. Instead of an immediate answer, she thinks for a moment, and then says, "You're right. I'll have to think about that." This feels like a huge moment. Me, challenging a definition put forward by the very person who birthed the modern intersex movement. This must be huge. This must mean something important to me, too, about my identity. Maybe this is the moment I've been waiting for, when my identity is finally recognized and confirmed.

But that's not the way life works. And especially not with intersex. That moment was all it was. It was certainly significant in that my other fear wasn't confirmed: that Cheryl would say, "Well, Thea, you're really just not intersex." No, she didn't say that. So I was left thinking that I am intersex, but that the definition that often got put out there didn't necessarily sound like it included me. Based on this definition, I feared that people wouldn't believe I was intersex.

What I can tell you now, years later, is that this definition, and my fears of exclusion because of it, are all based on the assumption that 1) people will even consider doubting I'm intersex when I claim I am and will be looking for proof, and that 2) people have an idea what my genitals look like. Now that I've realized that my identity and my experience aren't up for anyone else's confirmation or approval, I'm a lot less nervous when I tell people I'm intersex. I also know the ways in which my experience isn't the same as other people with intersex, so people shouldn't assume anything—genital conformation or life experience—when they hear someone is intersex.

Back in Atlanta, I feel excited about this conversation with Cheryl and search for someone to discuss it with, but it feels like everyone's having their own experience at the conference, their own drama, and I never really find a confidant. It's Saturday night, and the group does its first nonconference activity together. We go to dinner. I'm hugely relieved that we're finally all in one place being social rather than meeting about fundraising or for some other organization-building purpose.

Besides that quick, informal dinner with four of us from the first night, this is the first time I get to really talk to and meet with the other intersex people at the conference, and really to meet with other intersex people in a group setting. They are remarkably different from each other. There's one woman, a professional in her late thirties, who's dropped by for the dinner. She's chatty and smart, and tells me about her condition, how she's going deaf from it, and about several of her other health problems. This is really different from Lynnell, who was "given" surgery and raised as a boy, and who suffered abuse at the hands of her mother because she was never masculine enough. She transitioned later on to become a woman. She has no health problems that I know of now and lives as an intersex leather dyke. Natalie is there. I'm dying to get to know her because she lives in San Francisco and seems the most like me in terms of her community of friends. Also, I'm intrigued by her: she seems wicked smart and mysterious and funny.

It's not easy to talk to her. She alternates between ignoring me and teasing me in a sort of aggressive way that I can keep up with, but doesn't leave much room for any real conversation. After a while, I give up and talk to the other people at the table. The dinner takes forever to arrive, and we write add-a-line haikus, passing the poems around the table for everyone to contribute.

After dinner, I'm ready to go out. I envision a cadre of intersexuals taking over the local dyke bar. We have our ISNA T-shirts on, after all. Everyone at the conference was mentioning a lesbian bar called My Sister's Room. I try to drum up energy to get the group to go, but to no avail.

We get back from dinner in time to make the conference open mic. There aren't a whole lot of people there, but I read, and Lynnell and Ana do too. The one person I really want to hear me read is Natalie. I want her to see where I come from, be as impressed with me as I am with her. She never shows up, though. I do see the cute girl from the Boston LGBT anti-smoking nonprofit. She'd been at the ISNA presentation earlier, and she wants to go dancing at My Sister's Room. Her name is Andie, and she's willing to drive. I barely know her, but I figure, what the heck.

We go out that night. And stay out until 4 a.m., dancing and drinking. Andie is a few years younger than me, with a baby face, short hair, and preppy boys' clothes—a combination I find very appealing. I flirt with her outrageously, getting her to hold my wallet "like a boyfriend would." She's very shy and seems overwhelmed. I'm in love with the dance floor in this place: it's made of marble, it's outdoors, it has a disco ball hung above it, and it's about twenty-five feet from the train tracks. With perfect synchronicity, a train goes by in the middle of a song with a driving beat and the two sounds, the music and the train, meld until they're just a rhythmic pulsing coming from the ground and the air around us. I'm easily seduced by Southern hospitality: some local girls buy me drinks, a local boy gets me stoned, and I end up dancing with four or five different girls by the end of the night, including the DJ, who notices that I don't seem to be from around there, and tells me she just moved to Atlanta from San Francisco. At last call, I find Andie, and we drive back to the hotel.

Sunday morning's ISNA preconference meeting arrives way too soon. I've had four hours of sleep and I'm probably still drunk, if not a little stoned. It's 8 a.m. Everyone is teasing Natalie about flaking on the open mic, but, more importantly, on the girl who showed up at the reading to take her out. They keep telling her, "Hey, you flaked on Andie last night," and I figure out that this is the same Andie who took me out last night, and who must have taken me out when Natalie didn't show up. And who gave me no play whatsoever, despite my best efforts. I'm feeling kind of weird because Natalie was the one person who I really wanted to show up at the open mic last night to hear my work. And then I ended up going out with the girl who wasn't really interested in me, but actually had a crush on Natalie.

Mark tries to console Natalie for missing her chance with Andie. "If you'd known she was coming back, you would've come," says Mark.

"Yeah, I would've come," says Natalie, smiling. From the way she and Mark are talking, I think they're joking, making a sexual innuendo about orgasms. And so I tell Natalie—jokingly, because I don't think shy Andie would've put out for anyone, even her—"No, you wouldn't have." And I get a weird look and silence from Natalie.

Natalie seems angry during the meeting and won't meet my eyes.

I ask her later if she's offended that I went out with Andie, and tell her that I hadn't known until that very morning that Natalie was supposed to meet Andie at the open mic. And Natalie replies that actually she thought my joke was kind of rude. And she looks at me, real close and bitter and sad and says, cattily, "Because I can't come." Her hand is on my face, sweet almost, and then she slaps me lightly and says, "But you didn't know that, did you?" and stalks off.

The fact is, I do know that she can't come. Because of the surgery she's had, one of the many awful results is that she can't come. I simply just misunderstood: I thought she and Mark were joking about sex, but they definitely were not. Natalie thinks I made that joke about not coming with Andie as a way to tease her about her inability to orgasm. I would never ever intentionally point this out or joke about it. But Natalie doesn't know me well enough to know that.

Truth is, I would never make fun of Natalie. I actually find her an incredibly sexy person and have had a crush on her long before the conference. Natalie and her body and her amazing politics have been haunting me for weeks. Natalie embodies the intersex experience for me, and my mind wrestles with her as a way of figuring out my own relationship to intersex. She floats behind my eyelids during sex with my new girlfriend, appearing like a secret lover, surprising me when she appears there, shadowy and knowing. In the middle of sex, I think of her and wonder, what part of this do I take for granted? And I think, where would Natalie want me to touch her? And I think, where would she touch me? And I think, at what point does she tell a new girl? And I think of her too much, but only because I'm just trying to figure my self out.

Swallow

I went to see my doctor this week. I have stopped taking birth control, which I have taken for the last eleven years, and I recently reduced my dexamethasone, in an attempt to be as much me as I can be.

With the pill gone, I've started breaking out on my face, neck, hairline, and back. The same places I broke out all during high school and college. I have noticed long hairs on my upper lip. More on my cheeks. And not the regular long peach fuzz. I was concerned that these changes reflected a change in my chemistry, in the amount of 17 hydroxy progesterone getting turned into testosterone. And I've asked my doctor, and he says it's hard to tell. He can never account for a causal relationship between my hormone levels and my symptoms, especially if it isn't reflected in the lab tests. And so far, it hasn't been.

I stopped taking medication the first time after I went through puberty at age thirteen. My endocrinologist said I didn't really need it anymore since I had probably gotten all the height I was going to get. He said the only reason I'd be taking it now would be for cosmetic reasons. But by the time I was seventeen, my acne was bad and my periods were abnormal, so I started up on the medication again and have been on it ever since.

More than a decade later, I'm learning about intersex and meeting people that are on no medication at all, even people who have my condition—they took no medication at all. My whole life, my CAH has been discussed as a health problem. But now I realize it's a sex problem as well. To what degree have I taken medication to maintain girl chemistry, to attain girl attributes and keep boy ones suppressed?

To what degree have the doctors done this, and in what ways have I become complicit? My medication suppresses the overproduction of 17 hydroxy progesterone, a precursor to testosterone. What else is being suppressed? It made me wonder what would happen if I wasn't on medication, and made me wonder what else I'd been swallowing along with all those pills.

Present

I went to Queeruption. I wasn't going to go. My new plan was to avoid this queer anarchist conference that I had been helping to plan and organize for months. Mostly I wasn't going to go because seeing my long-distance ex-girlfriend there the first night, with an ever-expanding colony of hickies, made my eyes sting and stomach turn. Oh, and it made me hate myself for wanting her. Despite the reasons not to go, the reason I went was that there was a workshop I wanted to go to. And there was one on intersex that I was co-leading.

The workshop was on trans inclusion and activism in women-only spaces. I've always been aware of the inequities of women-only spaces, such as the Michigan Womyn's Music Festival and Osento, the women's bathhouse in San Francisco. What's changed recently is my connection to trans issues: the trans umbrella that I find so inappropriate for me as an intersex person does offer me shade, support, and community. I don't feel comfortable going to the Michigan Womyn's Music Festival; I think it would be too painful to be torn between my friends inside the festival and those, literally, across the road from it in Camp Trans. I don't go to Osento anymore, either. I went to the workshop because I wanted to know how to talk about the issue of women-only spaces and trans inclusion. And I went because my girlfriend is slowly but surely—and, it seems, inevitably—moving toward fully embracing a trans identity. She lives the fear and confusion of it everyday. She speaks of herself as transgender, and she's wrestling constantly with the issue of those breasts and whether to get them removed; and if yes, how; and if yes, when, before or after the baby.

So, high-strung, stressed, and dressed as a high-femme, I attend the workshop with my girlfriend. During the initial go-round, I introduce myself as intersex and receive nods from the boys named Dana and Cooper. I say it like I say my number at the gym, knowing it'll gain me entrance, instant cred in a discussion I barely have the words for, within a larger society that allows me to pass often and with ease. I don't know why I introduced myself that way. I guess I needed it, a reason to be there when I couldn't stop fidgeting, looping the rubber band I was holding in tighter and tighter nooses around my purpling thumb, appreciating my girlfriend's presence, feeling nervous because she'd never met my ex before, the ex I was still getting over. Knowing my ex, I had a feeling she'd be at this workshop, and I found myself feeling somewhat put-off at times by my girlfriend's arm heavy around my shoulders, holding my hand, then feeling bad because her affection might have been out of need rather than possessiveness.

When my ex did walk in, she chose the empty seat next to my girlfriend, poor thing—as usual, in the space between my ex and me.

What I did next was move back so I couldn't see the ex. And then I moved closer to my girlfriend. And what I did next was try to really think about what I could do to bridge the communities I'm in: trans, queer, women's, performance.

What I got from the discussion is that everyone is scared for their physical and emotional safety. And that we probably don't know the extent of the other's fears or needs. We need to listen first, without an agenda. Without anything besides trying to understand the one we don't agree with.

Within this discussion about safety and bodies and space, me and my girlfriend and my ex talked. Not to each other, but around each other and to the group. My ex referred to something I said, using my name, and I thought, how dare she, and also I loved it, and my girlfriend quieted my frantic fingers by gently holding my hand.

What I didn't like about the discussion was that not everyone in the room talked, and some of us talked a lot. I didn't like the tension of not wanting to look at my ex, even while she nodded in my direction. I didn't like watching my girlfriend try to be extra articulate while in the same room as my ex, or watching my ex's hands pick at each other in her lap. And I didn't like not knowing who I was protecting, me or my girlfriend or my ex.

What I loved about the workshop was that no one yelled and no one walked out. People were trying hard to be clear and kind. I got excited when one gay man read his list of what he was going to do to work for trans inclusivity back at home, and then other people did the same. I loved, in a perverse way, that I was in the bathroom so I didn't see when my ex turned and introduced herself to my girlfriend. My friend Amber told me they shook hands, and I picture those hands touching, slim long fingers grasping slim long fingers, fingers that have been achingly deep inside me. I loved that in leaving the workshop early I got to kiss my girlfriend and then walk past my ex, seemingly—only seemingly—ignorant to the twist of her shoulders and her gaze my way as I left the room.

The next day, I told my story for the first time. I co-led a workshop with two other intersex activists, Hida and Xander, called "Born Queer: Intersex: Fucking with the Sex and Gender Program." I don't know who came up with the title. I understood it, but at the time I might have called it something more like, "Intersex Awareness & Activism." Today, I usually title my talks something like, "Intersex Makes for Great Dinner Table Conversation."

At Queeruption, I was too nervous to assert much of anything. I was nervous to tell my story: how I was diagnosed, what my life's been like, what makes me intersex...mostly I was nervous because I wasn't all that sure if I was intersex fully, and because the group I was speaking to was so politicized. Hida, Xander, and I all had different definitions of intersex. At the time, I defined it as someone born with anatomy that someone decided wasn't standard for male or female. Hida disagreed with my definition because the definition itself referenced another's standard of the intersex person's body. She pointed out that her body, particularly her very large clitoris, was not the standard for male or female regardless of whether "someone decided" it was or not. She said she was fortunate to have escaped surgery or other medical "decisions" about her body, but that this did not negate her being intersex. She felt the definition should be "people born with anatomy which is not standardly male or female." Xander considered intersex an identity outside of the gender binary. I considered it a set of shared experiences of sex and gender oppression. I understood the problem of basing a definition on treatment by others, but that common oppression was all I understood as an organizing concept at the time.

The workshop took place in a warehouse space in North Oakland. A ragtag group of queers were there, people I can't remember now, but many of whom have come up to me over the years to tell me they were there. At the time, I just knew that even though I was surrounded by friends, I could say the wrong thing at any moment, something that would expose me as not what I was claiming to be, or something that proved I wasn't all that radical. Which, in comparison to my peers in the workshop, I wasn't.

Hida started with her story. She had grown up feeling different, more aggressive than other girls, her mother, her sister. In college, she started sleeping with other women and comparing her body, and she realized her body was different too. She never felt there was anything wrong with being intersex, and she was never diagnosed as having any kind of medical condition. I was amazed by Hida's composure as she told her story: she was honest and funny and didn't seem nervous at all.

I told my story next. I talked about being nervous because I'm still trying to figure out what parts of my experience are about maintaining health and which are about maintaining gender. I said I was thinking of going off my medication. I spoke about how my mom caught my condition early, that I always felt proud of being special, but also that I was aware that my difference or freakishness originated from my genitals. I talked about how 40% of girls with my condition end up being bi or lesbian. I don't remember looking at people's faces as I spoke. I don't remember what it felt like to tell the story. I remember trying hard not to look at my ex, who had come to this workshop as well.

When I finished, Xander said he wasn't comfortable with the language I was using, like "condition" to refer to CAH or "should have" when I said my body "should have produced one enzyme and didn't, so another enzyme overproduced the precursor to testosterone." While I agreed with him, I felt really embarrassed. I felt exposed, my language clearly reflecting the experience of having a body that had been pathologized and medicalized and described to me as the result of a mutation. But I also understand the problem with words like "condition." Condition is a polite way of saying something unpleasant, something you're stuck with that gives you gas, dandruff, or inappropriate genitalia. It's a euphemism for freak or hermaphrodite, the person becoming conflated with the affliction. Condition is something wrong, most likely uncorrectable, with the desire for normalcy implicit. Condition is also to train, groom, tune, lick into shape. To habituate. And that's where the word became more accurate for me: I've become accustomed to being different, broken in. I explained to Xander and the others in the workshop that I was just beginning to see my body in a completely new way, learning that my body was something to be appreciated and normalized socially, rather than fixed medically.

I don't remember the story Xander told that day. In my shame and excitement, I blanked out the rest of the afternoon. What happened that day was that I began to claim my experience as an intersex person, no matter how awkward or imperfect it might be. Soon, I'd come to know that that awkwardness, that feeling that there was some way to be that I couldn't quite attain, was one of the most intersex things about me.

Allies

I'm getting together the flyer for *Rated XXXY*, a performance event with all intersex performers. And while it's okay to say "all intersex performers" to myself, in my head, and while it's okay that Emi, in her email to me, described it as the world's first "all-herm show," I realized I can't do that on the flyer. For so many reasons.

The performers don't all identify as intersex. Plus "All Intersex Performers" sounds like a porn revue from Amsterdam's Red Light District. Plus, intersex isn't necessarily an identity and calling them "intersex performers" reduces them to simply that. Plus, intersex is a medical term. And mostly, I wasn't comfortable using it because it makes me nervous to lump people together under any kind of umbrella term.

Emi helped me rethink the descriptor line to "spoken word performances reflecting intersex experiences." And that felt better. The public/privateness of intersex, this constant negotiation between self-definition/representation and group representation, is eternally shifting and in dispute. This descriptor line allowed me to sidestep those quagmires.

Emi and I talked about the problem of language in our allied communities. About how problematic it can be when an intersex person says, "I never quite felt like a girl or a boy, but rather in between, something different," as an explanation for their intersex-ness. How does everyone else, the non-intersex people who never felt quite like a boy or girl, account for their difference? What's their diagnosis?

After an Intersex 101 we attended, my trans lover felt so torn. He was happy for me that I was finally getting information about myself and my history, my body being revealed to me with each new discussion I'd have or documentary I'd see. And he felt jealous. "I want a condition," he said. "I want a concrete reason I'm this way."

War

Being in love is the opposite of being at war.

At night, I pray for my beloved, counting down the days until her arrival. In the morning, I awake to an ever-increasing body count.

I take the war on terror personally.

America is killing people in the name of freedom. Freedom, the new f-word, a profane mantra spilling from America's mouth.

My beloved gave Hafiz to me, he gave the poet poetry. She reads me Hafiz when the distance pulls tight and our own words fail. Hafiz, your poems are little miracles that manage romance without making me wince.

I take the war on terror personally because America's idea of freedom is everyone having access to the same dream. Not the same access to resources, but access to looking like we have access to the same resources.

I send him small things found during the long days of waiting: a dried flower, lemon verbena, a sprig from the poplar tree down the street. We talk about marriage—or commitment, really, since marriage isn't an option. Since neither of us grew up thinking we'd ever get married, since we were always different.

I take the war on terror personally because the war on terror is really a war on difference, because my body strikes terror in the hearts of other Americans.

My body and the bodies of the people I love are the most intimate sites of American imperialism. Because our sex anatomy isn't normal, they operate on us without our consent. Because who we have sex with isn't normal, they won't let us get married. Because our gender isn't normal, they don't give us jobs, health care, or housing. We work, we pay rent, we pay taxes, but because we're not normal, we don't get the same freedoms other Americans enjoy, the same freedoms American soldiers are murdering to protect.

Normal is a weapon of mass destruction. It's just as deadly, and just like those weapons, it'll never be found.

I love San Francisco because we're not normal here, we're revolting. Every time we break an unjust law by marrying each other, we're revolting. Every time we declare the bathrooms in a building gender-neutral, we're revolting. I love San Francisco because so many of us are revolting everyday, just by being ourselves. Every time we choose an option that wasn't offered, every time we question, we make it safer to be in between, safer to be in the Middle East, safer to be an American.

Sometimes the longing for my beloved gets so sharp that I'd rather end it than continue. Sometimes the sound of her voice from far away feels like everything bad that ever happened. In these moments, when love is most dangerous, I want to run and I want to fight.

Hafiz, you urge us to rest because our separation from God is the hardest work there is. Maybe war is separation from love. Maybe longing is why war is even an option. Perhaps each of us, often, is at war.

I said to my beloved, "I want to write like Hafiz, but it's not working."

And he said, "You can't compare God to God."

If only they could see the poems she sends me.

I'm tired of resisting love. Love will never be safe, but we've seen the alternative.

Rather

Sometimes I think the way best to tell you who I am is to tell you how I make choices when there are two potentially bad options. On a radio show I used to listen to, they'd ask callers to choose between two evils: would you rather lick a four-inch section of a handrail or a one-inch section of a urinal?

I have several of these rathers: I'd rather be hit than tickled. I'd rather have a blood test than go to the dentist. I'd rather tell you about my masturbation habits than tell you my dad's in more trouble than Martha Stewart ever was. I'd rather tell you what my ex and I fought about than tell you I've worked forty hours a week at a desk job for the majority of the last ten years. I'd rather talk about anything than talk about class. And here's why: with class, no one wins, no matter how they identify, no matter how they're defined by others.

Class is all about shame. You get to feel it if you're working class. You get to feel it if you're middle class. You get to feel it if you're owning class. The queer community has done a pretty good job at celebrating diversity. My theory is, if we all didn't have so much shame and confusion around class, queers would be celebrating class the way we do everything else: we'd have class contingents at Pride. But you don't see the Working Class March, you don't see the Middle Class Float or the Owning Class Contingent. Of course, it could be argued that the whole Pride celebration is at this point one big owning class contingent.

Queers have been able to celebrate every imaginable status and oppressed group, but somehow, class kicks our ass. Class is so hard for communities because there's no better way to measure oppression than class and access or perceived access to resources. Capitalism is based on competition and comparison, more than/less than, and it's pretty much got us pitted against one another, feeling shame and confusion about what we have or don't have. Class is a trickster: the invisible coyote, a red herring. Class weaves its way into our fishnets, our bootlaces, under our fingernails, and into our beds.

When I moved in with my ex—this is before we were exes—there was a lot of conflict around class. Most of the stuff in the house was mine: the couch, the table and chairs, the rug. I was forever pissing her off by asking her to put something between her head and the couch when she laid on it. Her hair was fabulous, but it took a ton of greasy product to look that way and I didn't want oily spots on the couch. Of course, this came up in therapy, and I thought I had it all figured out, how she came from a working-class background, how I came from an upper-middle-class background, and how the couch was really a metaphor for power imbalances we played out. And then she got me. "You're so sure you had the privilege?" I remember her asking, turning to look at me across the therapist's leather couch. "Well, what about the fact that your dad lost everything and you had to move all those times? What about the fact that you had to rent a house?" She went on, "At least my single mom had the same job my whole childhood and we owned our own home. At least my childhood was stable."

I realized she was right. Class is a lot more complicated than it looks on the surface. It's complicated for me because I was born into an upper-middle-class family, but our financial status swung wildly and unpredictably. My class is also complicated by my religion, queerness, gender, and sex. Which is why I'd rather talk about global capitalism than talk about the fact that it's been butches who made rude comments to me about the neighborhood I grew up in and how much money my parents had. I'd rather talk about how fucked up the Bush administration is than talk about how class divides us and turns us against each other. But truth is, I'd rather talk about class than keep reinforcing the distances that grow between us when we don't talk about it.

I grew up in Oakland with progressive, upper-middle-class Jewish parents. It was the early 1970s, and my parents had to answer questions from relatives and friends such as, "Oakland? Don't the Black Panthers live there?" My parents were pretty unique. They both played the accordion. They had both hitchhiked through Europe, separately, when they were in their early twenties. And when they had me and my brother, they tried to raise us without gendering us, letting us play with whatever toys and dress however we wanted. Of course, my brother chose the guns and trucks, and I chose the animals and dolls. As idyllic as it sounds, there were repercussions to being raised with parents who themselves were caught between conformity and rebellion, between living the American dream and critiquing it.

My birthday is in January, right after Hanukkah. When I was eight, my mom became fed up with all the presents: I would get presents for Hanukkah, and then a month later I got more things for my birthday. It was unnecessary, she said; I didn't need any more toys; it was overdone, gluttonous. She didn't want me spoiled. So that year, for my birthday, she held a party for me, but she told the parents that their kids could bring me cards or flowers, but no gifts. It was my worst birthday ever. I felt awful: I wanted those presents! But I felt horrible for even thinking that I deserved presents when there were poor children who didn't get presents. I felt doubly guilty because I didn't need the presents, but I still wanted them. There was always a painful awareness of having things other children didn't have. There wasn't pleasure around money or things because there was always a shadow of guilt and shame.

Kindergarten through third grade I went to Oakland public schools. After severe funding cuts, my parents sent me to a private school, Head-Royce. To this day, I consider the three years I spent at that school to be the worst three years of my life. The kids were extremely aware of themselves as rich and entitled. I wanted to be as different from them as possible, and at the same time, I struggled to be cool. In fourth grade they all wore Lacoste alligator shirts. By the time I got my one alligator shirt, Polo was all the rage, so the alligator was out and the guy on the horse was in. I just couldn't keep up. Tight designer jeans were very important, but my parents didn't believe in them. And I couldn't fit into them, either, since I never was skinny enough. I finally gave up and began to define myself against the tide: I wore my El Rancho Navarro camp sweatshirt, baggy jeans, and Adidas.

I sported green, orange, or black nail polish and a safety pin in my ear.

I had two friends the whole time I was at Head-Royce. The three of us were the oddballs, the last ones picked on teams, the ones who read books during recess. The best friend I had at school was the art teacher, whom I would visit before school started each day. But here was the weird thing: all the most popular boys at school wanted to go with me. The kids thought I was a lesbian, whatever that was, but the boys were completely enthralled with me. In sixth grade, Robbie Wellstone gave me a dozen roses. All the attention from boys taught me being different is a curse but it can also get you noticed. I learned that even if you have few friends, you can have sex (or whatever passed for sex in sixth grade, namely, going together). I learned that sex can be more powerful than friendship. And that success means befriending those in power.

School was also where I learned that sex, or, more accurately, gender, and I mean specifically my gender as a socially appropriate-appearing girl, could sometimes be used to get things I wanted. There's no better illustration of how I learned about power and gender than getting on *The Tonight Show*.

Now, if you ask me, I'll tell you I grew up in Oakland. I'd rather tell you I grew up in Oakland, but the truth is, I also lived in Piedmont from age thirteen to eighteen. Piedmont is a very wealthy town in the middle of Oakland. Piedmont is the home of the Leonard J. Waxdeck bird-calling contest. Piedmont is also home to a long-held tradition of high school sororities and fraternities with puking parties and hazing rituals that would shame any town, but of which Piedmont couldn't be prouder. Piedmont is where a friend of mine who happens to be a woman of color recently got pulled over when she drove through town.

When we moved to Piedmont, I decided I was going to be one of those kids that get to be on TV. My family had been watching the bird-calling contest for years. By my senior year, I hated Piedmont, and I had stopped working the system there, stopped trying to look like all the rich girls. But I also knew that Mr. Waxdeck (you can guess the nickname we had for him), the teacher in charge of the bird-calling contest who chose the kids to go to *The Tonight Show*, liked nothing more than a pretty girl. I agonized about what to do. I had my birdcall down, my speech memorized, but I knew I'd have to do something to get his attention because I wasn't known as a pretty girl.

The week before Mr. Waxdeck would be choosing who went on Carson, as he called it, I started wearing skirts and makeup. Monday morning, in Marine Seminar class, first thing Waxdeck said was, "Ms. Hillman, you look very nice today. Maybe there's a chance for you on Carson after all." He asked me to audition later that afternoon. My birdcall was perfect: speech, flawless. He said I'd be going. And then he asked me if I could get my braces removed in time for the show. I said no.

Going to Carson, riding in a limo, and meeting Sammy Davis Jr., was one of the most exciting experiences of my life. I learned I could pretend to be a pretty girl, even I didn't feel like one. Today, I can tell you it felt like drag. I didn't know that then. I just knew it could be very useful.

My ability to pass and my confidence grew, especially with my first job out of college. Well, my very first job out of college was as a valet parking cars at the Marriott. My second job happened because I published an erotica magazine. My co-editor had a friend who worked at a publishing company in San Francisco who designed the magazine for us. We picked her up at work one day; she was wearing jeans and a T-shirt. I decided that when I graduated, I wanted to work in publishing because I could wear jeans and a T-shirt and work with words. And that's what happened. I got a job at that company. For the first two years, I kept waiting to get fired, for someone to figure out I was queer, and a pervert, and certainly not cut out for corporate America.

What I found was that corporate America was much different than I thought. I was treated better than at any previous job, including working as a radical direct action community organizer for ACORN, where I worked twelve hours a day, six days a week, for $12,000 a year. Corporate America recognized my leadership and writing abilities, and supported me in learning new skills. I even got paid time-off to do volunteer work. I also learned that in corporate America there were much weirder people than me.

Each job I've had has taught me that I have access to a wide array of careers. And each relationship I've had has taught me how very precious that is. With the exception of one lover, my queer long-term relationships have all been with trans or butch people who didn't go to college. In each case, it wasn't a financial choice: it was because they felt they couldn't handle it or didn't feel smart enough. Some of them started life with more money than me, but economic status is fleeting, it shifts and changes, minute-to-minute, decision-by-decision.

To understand why I have what I have and what I have access to, I have to look at how I fulfill society's expectations and how I am rewarded for that. My appearance as a girl is as successful as it is because of decisions my parents made when I was just a toddler. After my diagnosis by doctors, my mom went to medical libraries to find out more about what I had. Her college education made this possible and made her feel she had access to this information. She wanted me to be normal so my life would be easier, so I would have access to the things that could make me happy. I underwent hormone treatments for the next twenty or so years to make sure I turned into a normal girl. My parents gave me an exterior that allows me to function and pass, no matter how freakish or different I feel inside. I know that had they not had the access to information and health care they did, I could have ended up very differently, with a body that would have made it more challenging for me to access whatever I wanted.

I've begun to ask myself where my drive to be middle class comes from. Is it so I can appear normal? So I can buy whatever I want? I haven't worked forty or more hours a week at a desk job because status or wealth is important to me. When my ex said my childhood was unstable, she was right. There was a reason I was always scared we might be homeless. From the earliest I could remember, my dad would tell me, "Things are bad, Thea." I knew he was talking about money, but he wouldn't answer any of my questions about what that meant. I had all the fear and none of the information. We moved repeatedly, and while I was in high school, my dad lost all the money we had. I knew nothing about money, but I knew we lost our house to the bank.

Several years ago, my dad lost just about everything again. But this time it was much worse. After he'd paid back the banks from the first big loss, he rebuilt himself and become a millionaire. I didn't realize how much money he had at the time because I was on my own, supporting myself. My parents felt strongly that they had worked for what they had and that my brother and I should do the same. We always had jobs when we were kids and looked down on kids who were spoiled.

My parents' plan was to spend the money they had in their lifetime. They just didn't always agree on how to spend it. My dad wanted to travel and support good causes. My mom, however, was incredibly uncomfortable with how much money they had, and she tried to give it away as fast as possible, creating a foundation for kids in war-torn countries and orphanages in Romania and Nepal. They never resolved their differences, but they didn't have to because the money didn't last that long.

What my dad didn't know was that his business partner was a con man so sly that his illegal business even fooled top-notch auditing firms. One day, when my dad was out of town, his secretary contacted him: the FBI was going through his office. My dad's business partner had run off to the Caribbean with millions of dollars—money that belonged to my father's investors, which included some of our friends, family, and my dad's closest business associates. My dad was left holding the bag. And it was a big, big bag. This scandal was one of the biggest financial scams in California history. My dad's name was published in papers all around the country, linking him to this guy who, the papers revealed, spent $50,000 on one dinner, was a drug addict, and—despite having a wife and two kids—bought his Las Vegas porn star girlfriend lavish gifts such as a grand piano and a house. Investors in this deal lost everything, including their retirement money and money for their kids' education. Hundreds of investors were angry with my father. He received death threats. Dad's lawyers wouldn't allow him to talk to his investors, so many family friends and relatives won't speak to him or the rest of our family anymore. After the civil suit was settled, there were criminal charges and my dad did indeed end up in prison. My parents' thirty-two-year marriage broke up. I didn't tell many people all this was going on. I wasn't sure how much of it had to do with me. I thought it was only my parents' lives that were affected, since my financial situation didn't change and I didn't have to move like they did. I also didn't think people would understand: Sure my dad had momentarily been a millionaire, but it was all gone now. Money gave my family the luxury of certain comforts, including important things like education. But it has also caused us a great deal of suffering.

For a long time, I thought it was good policy to hold off on telling people about what was happening with my parents, and my own financial status. By working all those years and saving my own money, I was able to buy a house in Oakland. I thought if I told people this, especially people I date, they might hate me or think I'm a sellout. That I'm not as queer or as committed to fighting against oppression for all of us. I've been scared they'd feel their queerness meant they couldn't get whatever kind of work they wanted. I've been scared they'd feel that my ability to pass means that I owe them, the same way the world owes them. Sometimes I'm scared that queers are taking the worst parts of heterosexuality—the myths about masculinity and control, femininity and financial submission—into our relationships. I've been scared that people will read my class and assume I have certain ideas about marriage and about how I want to be treated in relationship: namely, that I am a princess, that I want someone to buy me things, that I'm a pillow queen, and that I don't want to give any of those things in return.

Truth is, I've begun telling people my dad's in jail. And the majority of people I tell then reveal that they've had a family member in jail too. Or that they've survived some family scandal. And truth is, I'm beginning to attract people who think it's hot that I work hard and that I'm financially independent. I'd rather have balanced relationships no matter who's wearing the financial pants in the family. I want it to be as okay for queers to want money as it is for us to be downwardly mobile. I want us to see money and power as our tools, and not simply the tools of our oppressors. I'm still scared to tell you these things. But I would rather tell you than not, because I want us to have the life we've always dreamed of. Or I want us to start dreaming.

Education

Mom calls me from Florida. They're in the car: her and Uncle Buddy and Aunt Linda. I'm at work so we're catching up quickly, connecting about flights for my arrival at Thanksgiving, and Mom's stalling because Buddy wants to say hi but he's on another cellphone. She says, "Buddy wants to talk with you. He wants to say hello," and I say okay, but I'm thinking, I'm at work, and I'll see them in three days, and then she says, "We've been talking about intersex and ambiguous genitalia—he's really interested. I hope I did a good job. You'll have to fill in the holes. Do you have the video?"

I must be silent because she asks me again if I have the video. "Yeah, Mom, I have the video. That's great that you're talking about it." But I'm really feeling scared. The thought of feeling any more like a freak with my family than I already do is not appealing. I picture my family's attempt to deconstruct the intersex people in *XXXY*...and then me.

Mom is about to hand Uncle Buddy the phone when he picks up another call on his cellphone. I thank God for small favors.

Nightmare

I had a nightmare that I was preparing to go on TV to talk about intersex. I was representing the community and a bunch of people were leaving the room I was in, wishing me good luck, each person saying they had confidence in me. And I was desperately repeating one line over and over in my head, trying to remember the three root causes of intersex: hormonal, chromosomal, and, and.... over and over again. I kept trying to remember, and I felt the weight of unborn babies on my shoulders and all the intersex people I've met, heavy and wonderful. I knew I needed to come through for them. I woke up at one point and through the dream haze continued to repeat the causes, trying to remember the last one.

Privates

When I first started telling people about intersex, or telling them I am intersex, I would tell them it's people whose genitals present ambiguously as neither male nor female, or who have characteristics of both. And if I told them I'm intersex, I would feel compelled to tell them that my genitals appear "normal." Did I tell them for the sake of clarity, honesty, an admission, a confession? I think I needed to be affirmed as intersex in order to do the activism. And for that identity to be publicly acknowledged. There's this fear I have that people will think I'm just trying to be different, to get attention.

I would tell people that my genitals appear "normal," that my condition is slight, borderline, and that if I had it worse, I'd be a hermaphrodite. I had never said the hermaphrodite part until a few years ago, when I asked my mom, "Why were you so worried when I was little, when I had pubic hair?" She had told me it had been a very hard time, and I never understood what the big deal was.

"We didn't know what you had," she told me. "They told us you might be a hermaphrodite." Or maybe she said, "You could have been born a hermaphrodite." I don't remember the exact words, but I know that one time she used that word in relation to what I had and why they'd been worried. That's all it took: one time.

I tell people I started growing pubic hair when I was four, and they say "Wow," and are impressed, and I can put my intersex membership card back in my wallet. What makes me tell them I might have been a hermaphrodite, and that if I had it worse I'd be one... implying, of course, that I'm not? It's not shame so much as false modesty, in part, saying, "I haven't gone through what they've gone through." And fear, maybe: I'm more like you than I am like them.

And I've been thinking about how through my work I end up coming out in performance as intersex, and I wonder if every queer who's met me in the past decade or so is wondering what I have to offer, what bandwagon I'm jumping on, and why my name is on all those flyers for transgender events.

I'm not going to tell people about my genitals anymore. It's no one's business what my genitals look like. And it doesn't make a difference. If someone thinks I'm intersex, they are most likely going to think I'm different. Most likely they will never see my genitals, or ask about them. Let them guess, assume, imagine, fantasize. I picture some of them thinking I have a huge clitoris, dicklet, micropenis on my "femme" body. Some of them will get off on that image. Others may think, Well, that explains why Thea has always been such a freak. Others may be disgusted. And that's why I don't even want to wonder in the first place what others are wondering. Let them keep their thoughts private.

Out

When I started performing and presenting on intersex, it was like sorting laundry: choosing what to put in each load, what to separate, what to wash by hand. I had my quarters ready, my eco-friendly detergent, and my basket full of dirty clothes. I thought it was simply about darks and colors, a few themes, and what light to shed on each topic. I thought I was in control. And then everything turned upside down.

It all started out innocently enough. ISNA and GenderPac were going to hold a fundraising house party. ISNA had just finished the new training video and wanted to read a portion of the transcripts aloud as a way to inspire people about our work. That sounded pretty boring to me. Then Cheryl's partner Robin asked me if I wanted to perform, using the film transcript as inspiration.

She sends me a URL, a link to a secret place on the ISNA website where the transcripts were posted. There are hours of footage transcribed, nine tapes in all. Robin points me to a segment that was particularly powerful. Tape #3, "The Old Model."

What I read chills me. There are several people discussing the problems with the "old" model of treatment. First is a pediatric social worker's account of being called in to help calm a resistant patient who was receiving "vaginal dilation." There were all sorts of people in the room while the procedure was being attempted: a fellow in pediatric surgery, the attending physician, the attending special clinical nurse, two or three medical students. All the while they were holding the girl down, trying to insert something into her vagina. The social worker says she had no idea what she was supposed to do so she left the room and went to calm the parents instead.

Next I read a mother's account of having to dilate her six-year-old child after the child's vaginoplasty. Her daughter would scream, "Nooo," as her grandmother held her down while this woman attempted to do what doctors had told her she had to do so that when the child was older she could have sexual intercourse.

As I'm reading these accounts, I start to feel small and cold. The pulse of the screen and the walls of my apartment and the expanse of desk seem amplified. And me: I see myself reading at the computer, and I look tiny. What I'm reading feels wrong, like I shouldn't even be reading it, yet I read on. And I want to cry, but I don't, I just get tight, my throat constricts and fingers stiffly push keys so that I can keep reading.

Another pediatric social worker discusses the trauma of repeated genital displays. She says it's not the fear that's the most harmful, but rather the profound sense of shame and humiliation. That's the most disconnecting thing for human beings, to feel ashamed.

At this, memory takes over. I'm on the table at the doctor's office. I'm three, four, five, six, I don't know how old, I just know that every time I go to my endocrinologist's office, he feels my chest to see if I'm developing. This is not the part that I fear before every appointment. And it's not when he tugs down my underwear to see if I have any more pubic hair, and then pulls apart my labia to see if my clitoris is growing at an abnormal rate. The part I dread is when he touches my stomach, pressing in several places. He'd touch my stomach, feeling around, and I'd giggle convulsively. It tickled so deeply and completely that I couldn't keep still. The doctor would wait for me to stop being ticklish, would tell me to relax, and would try again.

And I felt bad. I would worry before each appointment that I wouldn't be able to stop myself from being ticklish. I would say sorry to him that I couldn't sit still. Only now do I see that this is the same little girl who apologized to the child molester, whom I was sure I had disappointed because I couldn't climb the tree in my skirt as he asked me to.

These memories aren't buried in some primordial mud of my mind.

What's buried are the feelings. I picture the little girl that's me bravely trying to keep still and not be ticklish. I wonder at her ticklishness. I wonder that she was never scared. That she never cried. That she never complained. That she never said no.

My mom was always in the room the entire time. The doctor was a nice man. I know this is true. But what I didn't know until now is that somewhere, hidden far away from everyone, and especially me, was a terrified person—and more particularly, a terrified little girl.

Over and over the words on the screen blur as my mind goes back to that office, to the big examination table, to the gowns that were too big for me because they were for adults, to the hairspray on the doctor's instrument tray that Mom and I always used to laugh about. It all looks sinister now. My mind skips to being seventeen, when my mom brought me to Children's Hospital. I'd been awake all night throwing up bile and I refused to go to school.

All day I waited in the doctor's office, then the hospital. I was given blood tests and asked questions. In particular, "Is it possible you could be pregnant?" They asked me this with my mom in the room, and then took her out of the room and asked me again. No one believed me when I told them I'd never had sex before. They thought I had a tubal pregnancy. At one point, a doctor gave me a pelvic exam. "This might feel strange," she told me. "This might hurt," she told me, behaving as if this was the first time anything like this had ever happened to me.

And the oddest thing was, and the thing that finally starts me crying right there at my desk, was that I felt like a slut when that doctor tried to reassure me. I felt dirty and too experienced for my age because I wasn't scared, because it wasn't new to me, because she had no idea, but this had been happening to me since I was a very little kid. Was I supposed to be scared? Why was this okay with me? Why wasn't I crying and refusing like my friend had during her first pelvic exam earlier that year?

None of those questions went through my head at the time. Only the emotions, which got quickly forgotten and then buried in the backyard of my mind in the rush of my emergency appendectomy an hour later. An ultrasound had revealed that my appendix had already burst in two, poison seeping into my body.

In the midst of all this remembering, my trans lover comes home, buoyant and happy after dinner with a friend. I ask him to come sit with me. He turns quiet when he sees my face. I tell him what I've been reading. "Why am I so ticklish?" I ask. "Why do I read this video transcript and feel damaged?" He says he's not surprised. He says simply, "I just feel like you're hurt." I'm still sitting at my desk, facing the computer, then turning to look at him, right into his eyes as he tells me, as my lover of over a year and a half tells me he has wondered if I'd been sexually abused but don't remember it. I'm incredulous. What? Me? Sex-positive me? The only girl I know with no shame, me? A sexual abuse survivor? I know it's not true, but why do I feel cornered, pegged, nailed? I look him straight in the eyes and then look away, scared for him to see me unscripted, to see more things I don't know or can't remember. I feel inside out in front of him and without answers, without information, without understanding of myself. How do you have a conversation about yourself when all of a sudden you don't know what you're talking about?

I feel hurt, but it seems awfully hard to justify. My treatment was a huge success. Everyone said so. I was never supposed to reach five feet tall. I was taller than they'd ever expected I'd be. I got my period on time. I could probably have kids. Then why did I feel bad? It wasn't like I'd had surgery like other people I knew. Or even a different-shaped body. Was I allowed to feel hurt?

My mind flashes back to all the intersex films and images I've seen over the past few years. The subjects of the films were people I'd heard about often and would end up meeting eventually. At the time, I felt so different from them. I had never had a body that others wanted to operate on to make it look normal. I had a determined sex that everyone agreed on, including me.

What didn't really register at the time, I realize now, was that while watching the films, I would get hot and flushed. A deep sense of shame, of feeling found out, would rise and swell and push up against my throat. A part of me recognized myself in those films. If it wasn't in the body itself, it was in sharing the name of the condition Congenital Adrenal

Hyperplasia, or seeing the clear disgust of the doctor, or watching a child being turned into a freak right in front of my eyes. Those things I shared. Maybe that's what being intersex was about. Maybe I didn't need to have had surgery. Maybe the most intersex thing about me was my experience of how my body was treated and how I felt, rather than whether or not I had confusing anatomy or genital surgery.

Still, with all this information, I didn't know how to act. Was I supposed to break down? Was I supposed to seamlessly integrate this new material into my fabric of self? I grabbed little scraps of paper and began to scribble down snippets of my conversation with my lover as we had it so that I could figure myself out later, when I was alone, when I had time to think. I had thought I was a shameless sex radical. I had thought I could have been a hermaphrodite. I had thought that other people with intersex were way more damaged than me.

Truth is, I had often felt like I understood sexual abuse survivors. I often felt a deep empathic connection. But doesn't every woman feel that on some level? I've felt deep empathy for people sleeping on the street, but I've never been homeless. So what was that sneaking, nagging doubt then? What was that awareness of another inside me?

I have a friend who's an abuse survivor. He told me he started dealing with his past hurts because he got tired of floating around the ceiling during sex. I'd like to float around the ceiling. A little flight would be good right now, a little release from this confusing body, this body that holds answers that will reveal themselves when my mind is finally up to hearing them.

Trust

What happened was my baby boy, not such a baby anymore, well, I needed to operate on him. And I thought I better do it myself. His testicles. I need to make the sack smaller. As he bounced on the bed, jumping off, making frantic circles from the bed to the ground and back, looking up at me with trust and so much fear in his eyes, I told him he was a good little boy for taking care to use his nervous energy this way. He asked me not to cut him, but I told him I had to. I searched through the instruction book, looking at the scrotal diagrams and dotted lines, snip here, fold there. It looked easy, but I was worried. Luckily, the book also included the utensils I would need, shiny silver clamps and scalpels, all lined up like new pencils on the first day of school.

Offer

I'm at work. I check my email. Something I do a million times a day. There's an urgent call for adoption for an intersex kid. A little Indian boy "with no teeth and no genitals" available by email. I check to make sure this isn't a joke, scroll quickly from the top to the end of the email. It's been forwarded to me from a friend at the International Gay and Lesbian Human Rights Commission and it's written by a human rights worker in India. The child was found "unattended in Delhi, wearing a red shirt and white pant and no shoes. His front teeth had fallen out." They are giving him away. They request an essay. They will give him to whoever has the best reason for wanting him. "He is active and attention seeking. He takes regular diet and like all other children, he is also fond of ice cream and sweets." They ask interested parties to email information about themselves and why they might want to adopt him. "He calls himself a boy and we don't want him institutionalized." He's free to a good home. I picture his small body strapped into a big airplane seat on a plane headed to the United States. The United States, where the birth of an intersex baby is considered a psychosocial emergency. Where thousand of babies' and kids' genitals are mutilated by doctors every year in the name of normalcy. "He calls himself a boy." Once he's in the United States they'll probably turn him into a girl. And they may operate to make him that way. I sit at my desk and try to imagine the kind of person who would adopt a kid over the Internet.

Getting an intersex kid over the Internet is one step below mail order brides. The sick cats at the SPCA have it better than this kid. Take Snowball for example, the cat whose paws were amputated because a child put rubber bands around them until they turned gangrenous. At least Snowball got her picture in a four-color glossy brochure. This kid gets an email, the same medium people use to pass on that stupid urban myth about the department store tricking a consumer into buying the hundred-dollar chocolate chip cookie recipe; three-year-old alerts about Nina Totenberg reporting that NEA funding will be cut immediately; and those god-awful holiday cards like the one my cousin sent me that took seventeen minutes to download, the one with the naked girls wearing Santa hats sitting in front of an open fire, whose breasts jiggle back and forth to the tune of "Jingle Bells."

I swear, I almost thought this email was a sign from God that this is my kid, that this is the one I am supposed to adopt, kidnap, whatever. My friend sent me the email because she knew I was intersex, but I wondered if she thought I might want to adopt him myself. Wondered where he would sleep in my studio apartment. Then there was a flash of thin arms and legs wrapped around my waist and neck as I held him close, walking down 14th Street on the way to Safeway. Then the thought of him with someone else, someone who would answer this email. Then the thought that this eight-year-old intersex kid needs to be saved from his saviors. I didn't know at the time that emails like this are common. That people all over the world are trying to give away intersex children.

Intersex babies are like witches, like bums, like abortions. They are the moment before, the freak, the mistake, the genetic error, the mutant, the Martian. Last year, a woman in Texas bashed in the head of her four-day-old baby who was born with ambiguous genitalia. I think of her in those four days. Why did she wait? Was she waiting like a nervous bride, like a kid on Christmas morning, like an expectant mother? Was it killing her, that wait, from the moment she saw her baby's genitals. Did she feel it like a swelling urge, a sinister, undeniable ache, the desire to rid herself of this demon child? Did she picture herself poisoning it, drowning it, strangling it, setting it on fire? How did she decide? Or was she taken by surprise, overcome by this overpowering, orgasmic wrenching that caused her fingers to curl around tiny ankles, grasp warm little legs, and then swing? Did she feel the force of a living and breathing almost nothing at all hitting a wall? How much blood does a tiny baby have and what kind of mark does it leave? And did she bother naming the baby? And why, for the appearance of normalcy, to get past the horrified doctors and nurses, and then home? And will she ever try again? Will they let her get pregnant again and will she ever have sex again? Knowing the possible result, the sin of her lust and the sin of chemistry and the sin of difference and the sin of sex and the sin of pleasure and the sin of variation and the sin of one moment, of conception, realization, the moments then of madness and murder?

How will she ever be forgiven for all of her sins? And why do I think she already lives in fear of a strict and unbending God? Because it's Texas and because some gods have made us in their image and then there are other gods that give us permission to maim and kill, operate and murder, all in the name of maintaining the fiction of happy, procreating males and females forever after.

In the call for adoption over email I was offered the chance to save a little intersex boy. Save him. I declined the offer. I wrote a poem. I deleted the email. I wonder who will make him happy and healthy. I wonder if they will do whatever it takes to make him that way.

Reshaping

The organizers of *The Vagina Monologues* at UC Berkeley asked me to tell you what I think the world will look like without violence against women. So many images flashed through my mind. In a world without violence against women, my friends Donna and Jordan and Rickie would be able to get health insurance. Molly would have been able to get an abortion without shame and fear and lying. Carlie would have never been raped. Nor would Rina. In a world without violence against women, Lynne and Karen and Brett would not have started their lives understanding that a cousin, a brother, a father, can touch their private parts. And me? I wondered, how would my world, my life, be different without the violence that's been done to me? That's when I realized the problem with writing this for you. Because I wondered, in asking me to write about a world without violence against women, when they said "women," did that word include me? Maybe not. When we talk about a world without violence against women, I'm not sure we're talking about the same world or the same women.

To talk to you about what my world will look like without violence against women, I have to tell you about the women I know. And I have to tell you about their vaginas. I figure it's only fair to start with my own.

When I was four years old, a doctor said I had a condition called Congenital Adrenal Hyperplasia, which is one of the conditions that result in intersex. Today, it's not really such a big deal that I'm intersex. It doesn't usually come up. But it did the night I saw the *Vagina Monologues*.

There I was, in a downtown theater in San Francisco, at the

Vagina Monologues starring Eve Ensler. I was surrounded by hundreds of women and a few good men, laughing, crying, stomping our feet, clapping so hard our hands hurt. We were mothers, daughters, secretaries, writers, construction workers, sisters, friends, and coworkers, all together, united in our status as women and girls. Then Eve told the VFT, a real life Vagina Fairy Tale, about a girl born without a vagina. She said one girl in Oklahoma told her she had been born without a vagina, and only realized it when she was fourteen. She was playing with her girlfriend. They compared their genitals and she realized hers was different, something was wrong. She went to the gynecologist with her father. On the way home from the doctor, in a noble attempt to comfort her, her dad said, "Darlin', we've got an interesting situation. You were born without a vagina. But the good news is we're gonna get you the best homemade pussy in America. And when you meet your husband, he's gonna know we had it made specially for him." Eve concluded that Oklahoma loves vaginas.

The thing is, I know girls who were born without vaginas. Girls born with a condition, an intersex condition, same as the girl in the story. One of my friends, Kath, was born with fully functional ambiguous genitalia and no vagina. She was born with sensation in her genitals, could enjoy touch, and experience sexual pleasure with her body just as it was. However, in our world today, it's standard procedure for girls with ambiguous genitalia like Kath to be given surgery as infants and a while later to undergo a vaginoplasty, surgery to create a false vagina. Kath was told she needed surgery in order to be a real woman, to enable her to have sex with a man someday. She had the surgery. And lost all sexual function. She can no longer achieve orgasm or feel sensation. Her false vagina leaks, gets infected, and is literally falling out of her body. She and her parents were never told that the surgery takes away sensation and the ability to have an orgasm. They were never told that the surgeries are experimental and that they often fail. And perhaps most importantly, they were never told Kath could be a real woman, whether or not she had a vagina.

I felt hurt when I heard Eve tell that Vagina Fairy Tale. It hurt to be in a place where I was supposed to feel safe to be a woman, but instead ended up feeling like I was in a place that was promoting violence against women like me. So I wrote to Eve Ensler. And I feel so honored and amazed to be here. Tonight we really are helping create a world without violence against women because instead of someone standing here telling you that story, I'm here telling you this story.

In a world without violence against women, the girls I know born without vaginas will grow up without surgery, without fearing doctors, without fearing their parents, and without fearing that no one will ever love them just as they are. In a world without violence against women, these girls and their families will receive information, counseling, support, and be taught acceptance of their bodies as beautiful and good. In a world without violence against women, these girls will grow up with the bodies they were born with, with the understanding that some day they may choose to have a vagina created for them, with the understanding that a vagina doesn't make them a woman, and with an understanding that we all need to embrace, that even if you are born with a vagina, that doesn't necessarily make you a woman either.

I know a girl who was born with a vagina, but she doesn't feel like a woman. I'm in love with her. She's my girlfriend. In the world we live in today, there are girls who grow up feeling that their outsides don't match their insides, that the gender they were raised isn't what they feel inside. Some people call this being a masculine female, or butch, or androgynous, or transgender. My girlfriend gets "Ma'am... Sir... Ma'am"-ed all the time. People stare hard at her chest, trying to figure out what she is. She never feels safe going into public restrooms. She can't even decide which one to use. She's been kicked out of the ladies room by security guards and fears violence from men if she goes to the men's room. She's scared that if she uses the men's room, someone will find out she's a girl, and she'll get in trouble, get beat up, or be sexually assaulted. She's often afraid to go to the bathroom by herself, and as much as it mortifies her, she asks me to go with her. Not being able to use a bathroom safely is violence against women. In a world without violence against women, whether someone is a man or a woman won't have to be universally agreed upon and recognized simply for them to be able to go pee.

I want to tell you about another woman in the world I live in. Her name is Cindy, and she's transsexual. Now, despite her penis, Cindy is more feminine than I'll ever be. She's gorgeous: men and women fall at her feet. But that's not the point. Point is, hundreds of women like her are killed each year, transsexual women who started out life as boys, even if that's not how they felt inside. You know these women, you know their names, they live and die in our neighborhoods. This last October, just thirty miles from here in the city of Newark, we lost Gwen Araujo, who at just seventeen years old was beaten and strangled to death. In a world without violence against women, people will understand that some women are born with genitals that are considered male, that's just how it is. In a world without violence against women, all women, including women born with what are considered male genitals, will be safe to walk the streets, day or night, without fear. In a world without violence against women, transwomen, crossdressers and bi-gendered people will be able to find work, housing, healthcare, and loving relationships. No one will harass them because they're not a real woman, or ask if they're a real woman, they'll just know.

When I dream of a world without violence against women, I see four women walking down the street holding hands. Three are wearing skirts. Under the first skirt is the vagina you've heard about all night. Under another skirt are genitals that would be called intersex, free of surgery, able to experience sexual pleasure. Under the third skirt are what's considered male genitals, or the place where male genitals used to be. The fourth woman isn't wearing a skirt at all—she's wearing baggy jeans that show boxers at the top. All four women are smiling. All of them are free. I dream of women who hold their heads high because they live in a world where difference is embraced, rather than corrected, fixed, obliterated, or erased. A world where I learn from the women and girls around me about the myriad, multiple, varied and beautiful ways of being alive: joyful, silly, loving, and light. Because if I dream it can really happen, and then if I share the dream with you, it just might.

Science

I'm listening to *Living on Earth* as I drive home from visiting a friend, and I hear a story about a fascinating new finding. There's a very polluted pond, I forget where. If I had to guess I'd say Canada or the Pacific Northwest. And this pond is 100% effluent from a pulp and paper mill. The water appears black, and if you put your hand in it, visibility is only one or two inches. Scientists didn't think anything could live in this pond until they found these little fish darting around, mosquito fish.

And they found the darndest thing: all the mosquito fish had these things called anal fins, which are used for mating and which usually only males have. The scientists then realized that some of the male fish had a black dot on them, which is a marking of a pregnant female. But these pregnant females also had the anal fin. The scientists observed these female fish displaying "inappropriate sexual behavior" as they attempted to mate with other females, and they noted that these females exhibited unusual aggressiveness. "They acted like little sharks," one scientist said.

I'd like to interrupt this story to tell you what my head hears when I hear stuff like this. On the radio. On TV. Wherever. When I hear things about unusual sex and gender, I get excited. My first thought is, Oh, more people understand! And then I get nervous. What offensive misconception are they about to propagate? And then I get indignant. What rubrics are these scientists using for male and female? What kind of scientists are they, anyway? Why is it only okay to call them scientists but not tell us what field, what their contextual knowledge base is? What is "inappropriate sexual behavior"? And who decides this? Was it that they were pregnant and attempting to mate, or that they were females attempting to mate with females? And since when is aggressiveness not a female trait? And do we all agree that sharks aren't feminine? End of interruption.

Inappropriate sexual behavior is—you guessed it—females attempting to mate with females. To illustrate the aggressiveness of these fish, one scientist put a piece of paper in the tank and the little fish bit a hole right through it. Do fish not usually bite through paper? Did anyone consider attributing these behaviors to being in captivity or being traumatized?

The scientists also noted that although viable, these mosquito fish populations reproduced in smaller numbers than other mosquito fish populations. Scientists searched for the cause of these mutations. The scientists found high concentrations of androgens in the water, "masculinizing chemicals," and one in particular called "andro." They hypothesized that cholesterol from the wood bark was converted into andro by bacteria in the water. They were interested in the concept of life-forms affected by or interacting with pollution. I, however, found the story about intersex fish interesting for other reasons. What those scientists found in that pool was a crystalline reflection of the so-called and unquestioned "scientific" view of intersex: a mutation, in this case caused by pollution—which makes it only dirtier and nastier than it already was as a sexual oddity. And the scientific view of queerness: the inappropriate behavior of those individuals who attempt to mate with their own sex, pregnant or not, the implications being that that behavior is worthy of intense scrutiny, be those individuals fish or human.

Femme

Her. It's a distancing technique, to be sure. The word short and far away. A call. A reference without direction, but with intent. Her would be fine if it were true, but her is an assumption made across a crowded restaurant, on the page, in the restroom. Her is an assignment, homework, gossip, a guess, a limitation. Being intersex makes her half-assed and incomplete, a cop-out, and the easier of two destinations. Her is one path out of many. An option. A state of mind defined more by articulation than genital presentation. Her is me not because you say so, but because I haven't come up with something better yet.

Masculinity is a bronzed trophy, a blank check, a pit bull puppy, unaware of itself, able to support its weight by the strength of its jaw. I'm really attracted to masculinity, especially my own.

There's a girl in all white walking up 24th toward Mission. She's just gorgeous from behind: white shoes, endlessly long muscular white legs—I mean, they do end, but it takes longer than you might think because the white skirt is so short. I'm sure I'm going to see her ass any minute, but her skirt is at that impossible length where it covers the bottom curve of her ass, but just barely. Her white jacket says baby phat in sparkling letters; her brown hair is bleached blond, pulled into a short ponytail. Hearing my sleek boots with the thin heels hit the pavement, she turns back and looks at me. I smile. She looks again and smiles this time—this is how I know she's not queer. I see the dark around her eyes, bruised or tired, I can't tell from the dim streetlights. In that moment, I want so many things: to make love to her, to give her money, to laugh with her.

If someone asked me, I'd tell them I'm an assman. Problem is, no one asks. Lenny Bruce has this whole shtick about what's Jewish and what's not: Pudding's Jewish, Jell-O's Goyish. Funerals are Jewish, weddings are Goyish. Italians are Jewish. Asses are Jewish. I'm a good Jew.

I had a lover who was very masculine. She mostly only dated femmes, but you know how it is after a breakup, anything goes, so after we broke up she dated a young genderqueer boy for a while. She told me it only went so far, said she didn't know what to do with his body. She said it was like when she was in high school and she used to kiss her butch buddies. They would kiss, but they just didn't know what to do with each other after that.

This lover told me recently, after she dated this genderqueer boy, that that's how she used to feel with me sometimes. Awkward, like high school, but not in a good way. Like she didn't know what to do with my body sometimes. Like my masculinity confused her. Like sometimes she felt emasculated by it.

I've been a training femme for several butches. At least that's what they've told me, that I was their first femme. Which was always confusing for me because I don't identify as a femme, even if that's what I look like to people. I didn't see what was different about these butches from others I'd dated who did date girly girls, nor did I understand what these butches wanted from me. They seemed to have some script that I hadn't gotten. In each case, they treated me poorly and came on too strong at odd moments. If I made a smart or sassy remark, they'd come back with a snide, "All femmes are like that."

Of course, masculinity isn't just who you fuck, or how you fuck, or that you want to fuck. But that's part of it.

I'd like to tell you that masculinity has nothing to do with hormones, that masculinity is some innate thing, something distinct from muscles or chemicals, but in my case, that's not quite true.

Due to being intersex, I got some high doses of those chemicals that our society believes turn boys into men. I mean, those same chemicals do a lot of other things, like help a body develop or go through puberty, things all of us need. I guess I just got extra.

There are a lot of stereotypically male things I do: I'm usually not the crier in a relationship. Often the hottest thing for me isn't getting fucked, but is fucking someone else: I have fucked boy-girls on pool tables, against jukeboxes, in bathrooms, and in another girl's arms. I'm quick to sweat, to build muscle, and I'm not really a natural when it comes to cuddling. But then again, all that's bullshit.

What's a normal girl? Who doesn't have masculinity in her? Who doesn't get off fucking girls in public spaces? There's no such thing as a normal girl, thank God, and especially not in our community.

Still, boys were always attracted to me from a young age, attracted to my being sexually aware, precocious, but also strong. I fought with them, played with them, talked back to them. They were simultaneously drawn to me and repulsed by me, unknowingly seduced by my masculinity, a glowing white cock too hot to touch.

Miscarriage

I have been a mother many times, but I have never been pregnant.

There was that one child, older than me. I picked her up in a bar. Her apartment was small. She leaned back against her headboard, smug and sexy. Her mouth went slack, eyes soft, when she pulled down the straps of my bra. She made a noise I didn't understand yet.

I am the mother she never had. There have been a few of us in her life, makeshift mothers who fuck away the pain, or cry trying.

It was only moments, but it was no longer just sexy. She buried her head in my chest, arms around me. Surprised, I held her close. Something happened to this girl's mother, my head told me. This girl hasn't had a mother in a long time, my heart told me.

I am only thirty but I have been a mother to many girls. Oh my sweet girls. I haven't saved a one of them yet.

I hold her. Tell her she's beautiful. Hold her and rock her when she's hysterical, heaving sobs harder than any I've ever cried and I wonder, How will I ever hold all those tears, how can I teach her to let them go, that they are part of an ocean, lapping a welcome shore? My mother's heart breaks for a baby that isn't mine and for a child I know I'll have to give up.

I hold many of them longer than nine months. I have never carried any of them to term. It's funny that miscarriage sounds so much like marriage, but without the promise, the ring, or a future.

Poor baby. She is older than me, but I see the beatings in her young eyes housed in an ancient face. It's the pictures that kill me, a knife twisting in my mothergut. She shows me pictures. She hands me her hurt like a beloved headless doll, oblivious to what it reveals, each year another scar. The baby eyes in the pictures give way to a hard teenage grin and a glint that makes me wince. Each year a pristine new dress hung off her, and the pictures look more progressively wrong than the year before, the boy peeking out from the girl that's getting beaten to death inside there, by her mother, by her.

I fall for the girl who takes refuge in her brother, in boyhood, the girl who sees her survival in a square ass and flat chest. Today my girls wear army fatigues, hooded sweatshirts, and briefs. Their shoulders curve to hide their chests. They get mistaken for boys on the street and in public bathrooms, but I see the little girls, invisible to others, but unmistakable to me. Bigger than me, they hear "Sir" all the time, but they'll always be my little girls.

I love their little boy bodies. I love their breasts. I put food on the table, I hold down a job, I keep the house clean. Each time I tell myself, this one, this'll be the one, I'm going to save this one. And she lets me in. She lets me touch her. She lets me in and I tell her I love her and I tell her how to keep a job, to feed herself, to succeed in the world. I tell her, I believe in you, you have something to offer the world, you have a chance. But motherless girls don't want to be nurtured, they want to be mothered. And they'll do anything to not grow up, and not let go. So with every word of encouragement, I cement her failure. With every hope, every word of support, I build the tower of expectation she's going to fall from. And then with every hurt and disappointment, I seal a future without me in it. For she is motherless, and I will necessarily lose her, she will necessarily grow up without me. I lose another baby. And maybe I try again, when the bleeding resumes.

Testosterone

Sometimes I think I'm really different from you. You see, the queerer I am, the more I think I'm different than everybody else. It's as if there's this scale of queerness, and each degree of queerness takes me further from other people, even from other queers. And since I'm intersex, I often feel like I'm at this frontier of queerness, one of the last survivors of the Donner party, having buried many of my intersex compatriot explorers along the dangerous journey, and having eaten the others.

Being a queer pioneer often means that I think you don't understand me. And not only that, but I think I don't understand you, either. As I learn more about being intersex and I stop taking hormones, and as many of my friends and lovers learn more about their transgender selves and start taking hormones, I often think we're moving even further away from each other. It hit me recently that that's just isolation talking, and shame, and fear, because I do, on some level, understand what my trans friends and lovers are going through. I know intimately what they're going through. I know what their bodies are going through. And not just because I've had sex with some of them.

I know because I've been a female-bodied person on T. You know, I swore, just a few years back, that I'd never use that term, T. It seemed too familiar; it reeked of a false intimacy, like a used-car salesman, like a person giving you a nickname when they barely know you. For a long time I had this feeling people said T because they didn't want to say "testosterone" out loud. It took too long, had too much baggage—you know, that baggage attached to men. I wondered if not saying the word testosterone fed into people's denial. When people around me used the term T, I felt like they wanted to remake it, as if changing the word, making it theirs, ours, would change what it signified. And I guess it did. And I guess that's why I love language. And especially why I love queers. But I swore I'd always say testosterone out loud, its full length in my mouth, and I don't know when I stopped doing that, because now it feels like I've been saying T for as long as I can remember.

For as long as I can remember and from way before then, when I couldn't remember because my brain was still developing, my body was different from what people expected. Because of testosterone. Even before I was born, some little glitch occurred, some switch was pulled that would affect my body and the way my brain is wired.

As a four-year-old, I had a body that most likely caused people anxiety if they caught a glance in restrooms, in the changing room at the pool, at school. Which is an experience not unlike the experience of every butch and trans person I've dated for the last ten years. Except that I was a little kid.

Deep in my body, the body before conscious shame, the body before conscious sex, I think my body knew that it shocked people. I think my body scared the adults around me. I think my body bespoke of desires no one's supposed to have at that age and that no one in society is supposed to have for or associate with a child that age.

Today I can tell you those flashes of unexplained tension and anger I had as a young child were surges of testosterone running through me. Sound familiar? Flashes that no one knew to look for and that no one could understand. I wonder if I know, from before knowing, what it feels like when you get your weekly shot. I wonder if my body doesn't know the surging pulse of energy that makes you want to fuck everything in sight or hit something or double over because it's all so intense.

I know what it's like to develop muscle faster than the other girls. I know what it's like to run your hands over your thighs, feeling their hardness, watching the definition lines appear with less effort than before. I know what it's like to find those thicker hairs on your face, although I probably give them a less ecstatic welcome than you do. I know what it's like to have acne that's not attached to a period in your life when everyone's reading *Are You There God? It's Me, Margaret*, and wondering what sex is like. I know the feeling that something is coursing through your body that's making you different from the people around you. I know what it feels like when some people want to fix you, some people want to fuck you, and some people just want to cry.

And I think I know that feeling, the queerest one of all, sickening and soaring, a kite, a bird, a falling rock, the stone in the pit of your stomach. I understand the feeling that maybe you have too, the knowledge that for longer than I can remember I've had desires larger than my body could contain.

Community

When it comes to talking about trans and queer community, there are a whole bunch of things I can't say. In fact, it's much easier to think about what I can't say than what I want to say. Things I can't say because I will piss someone off: no generalizations, of course, about anything, but specifically, and most dangerously, no generalizations about transmen, transwomen, butches, femmes, genderqueers, or intersex people. I can't talk about my ex because you know him. I can't talk about my previous ex because you know him too. And if I do happen to talk about my ex, and call him her, as I did when we were together and as he's fine with, there will probably be someone out there who thinks that's not quite right either. I fear that regardless of the fact that I've been hormonally altered since age six in order to achieve and maintain a mythical gender ideal, I can't safely talk about my concerns about hormones and surgery in our community for fear of being seen as anti-trans and anti-surgery.

I can, however, talk about my dog. But I will do that only by qualifying it with the information that as of a year ago, I had two cats, and I used to be a cat person, just so you know that, if you're a cat person, I'm on your side. But truth is, I had my dog spayed recently. And don't you know, a few people who know I'm an intersex activist called me on giving my dog an unnecessary medical intervention.

I'm going to try to talk only about myself. And my experience of our community, as it were, which I would loosely describe as a bunch of people who have fucked each other or each other's girlfriends, read each other's writing, written about each other on Craigslist, seen each other perform, idolized, fantasized about, and recognize and sometimes even say hi to each other on the street. We're a group of people whose misunderstanding of each other is only topped by people's misunderstanding of us. And in the end that's probably what brings us together: our otherness, our queerness. And maybe what pulls us apart is the unquestioned assumptions about similarities that don't exist. That we should be able to relate to each other because the world lumps us together. It's like new lovers who have gotten beyond the honeymoon stage, who finally crawl out of bed to meet each other's friends and realize there's all this stuff they don't know about each other. And when we want support from this queer community, I think we forget that maybe we haven't actually taken the time to get to know each other, before we get pissed that others don't automatically understand us. Our community, like our lovers, can't automatically know our needs, or be able to meet them.

So, when it comes to talking about trans stuff, I'd like to use "I" statements. I'd like to tell you about myself, tell you my story. But that's impossible. Not because I'm not transgender—because by some definitions I am—but because I can't tell my story without telling yours.

I'm going down on your cunt (which to you is your balls) while smelling your sweat—which is all man, thanks to the T—and I come up for a kiss through the chest hair between your breasts that aren't long for this world.

Later, you show me pictures of what you looked like before T, from when we first met. From when you showed up at one of my readings and smiled at me the whole time from the back of the room. From years before now, now when I know what it's like to make love to you, the smell of your cunt and masculine sweat hotter than I ever could have imagined. My eyes linger too long on one photograph from back then. Way too long. You catch me and turn the page quickly. I feel guilty. I'm not supposed to long for that face. I feel I'm betraying the face I'm holding and kissing, the one I'm loving now, but I'd be lying if I didn't admit that something in me misses that person.

I'd like to tell you that for me, transgender is only about love, connection, and sex. But that's impossible. The thing I haven't wanted to talk about, the thing that makes me feel like a traitor, is that I can't tell our story without talking about longing, and loss.

For me, nothing symbolizes this loss like the names. Catherine. Karen. Kristi. The girls who are gone forever. The girls who never were girls. Heidi. Mary. Missy, Brittany, an endless litany, each one a seashell from a long-forgotten visit to the ocean, the living thing that once inhabited the shell long gone, dead, or moved on to a better-fitting home. I hold these shells in a mason jar, in basket by the bathtub, precious and dull now, farther each day from the water of birth, but still beautiful.

Sometimes I feel like I'm holding these names like their mothers do, remembering the bright baby girl. Other times, I hold their names like their first girlfriend would, the one in high school, the girlfriend that was probably a best friend, but in love, grateful for the first taste of masculinity in a woman's kiss—or so we thought at the time. Other times, I hold their names for them, a letter to a long-ago love, no forwarding address, marked return to sender, waiting in my kitchen drawer for safekeeping, for the possibility that someday they might want it back, or that they might just want to know it's being held.

Sometimes I want to string these names like worry beads on a necklace—not a warrior's proud display, but a grandmother's birthstone ring—each of these names a promise, a community secret, a secret handshake, as if San Francisco is one big clubhouse with a sign that says, girls keep out.

The boys at the BBQ are not outside, they are not gathered around the grill starting fires and flipping tofu burgers; they are inside, gathered around the computer, scrolling through a local surgeon's "before" and "after" chest surgery shots, their voices excited, unknowingly resembling teenage girls flipping through fashion magazines.

I'm drawn to these transmen as the unborn part of me. The medically unaltered self, the body no one wanted me to have. But as much as the results of their medical modifications touch me and turn me on, their choices scare me, especially their reliance on medicine to give them the body they always wanted, that no one wanted them to have. Their love-hate relationship with the needle and the knife, their worship of its power to give shape to their desire scares me because it's the same needle and knife that have sculpted my own dented self-image and stolen the desire from so many people I love.

As a young child with intersex, I was well acquainted with the needle. I had countless blood tests, sometimes several a day, to monitor my hormone levels. My genitals and breasts were examined by doctors, my height and weight measured often. As a child I had doctors telling me I had to lose weight in order to postpone precocious puberty. It became clear to me that my body, and my sexual organs in particular, were the origin of my freakishness. I spent a lot of time comparing myself to other girls to find out what was wrong with me and to figure out how to be normal. I learned to hate my body. And I learned to see my body as doctors did, adopting a view of my body as pathological and in need of medical cures. Today it's often hard for me to watch my trans lovers scrutinize their bodies, obsessively comparing their bodies to others, and turning to doctors in their efforts to realize their gender and sex.

As an intersex activist, I've been horrified to see my heroes, the Salvation Army of doctors from my youth, fall from their pedestals. I've been shocked by the damage inflicted on children and adults by well-intentioned surgeons. While I've heard one or two positive stories, I've mostly listened to my friends tell the disastrous results of their genital surgeries, seen barbaric film footage of clitorectomies deemed a success by the doctor, but in which the tiny three-year-old girl pulls fearfully away from the camera. From meeting them at conferences and medical meetings, it has been my experience that the surgeons who do genital surgeries are at worst arrogant and at best ignorant. At one such conference, Cheryl Chase was thanked for educating the surgeons about the importance of the clitoris for women's sexual function.

Transgender and surgery are also about power for me, loss of power. On an irrational, visceral level, I hate that surgeons touch the bodies of my lovers. I hate that they hold the solution. Maybe as much as some of my lovers hate that a man can get me pregnant and that they can't, I hate that I can't give my lovers the body they want or even the gender they want, that my love of their body, our sex, our queerness doesn't enable them to have it or to realize it.

Here are two final stories. Yours and mine.

I'm at a sex party with my lover. She gets busy with a guy with long ringlets, a beard, and yellow ducky underwear. It's not my scene, so I sit back and watch. And am completely shocked when I see Sarah walk in, an activist from the Transgender Task Force. I've always thought Sarah was the perfect woman: redheaded, green-eyed, she even cried a little when nominated as chair of the task force. She asks if I want to play, and I do. Her body is muscular and so soft. I'm amazed at her breasts, the strength of her biceps. My lover looks over and decides this is too hot to pass up, so the both of us make love to Sarah, kissing her, telling her how hot she is. Neither my lover nor I have touched a flesh-and-blood cock for years, but there we are, fucking Sarah's ass and pulling on her penis, which is hard, despite the hormones. She tells us she's going to have it removed in spring. She comes, a deep, body-rocking orgasm as we both hold her. She cries. We talk a few days after. She says no one had ever made her feel like we had. That she was beautiful just as she was, that we wanted her, all of her. Not for what she could do for us. And she told us she was considering keeping her penis. That she'd never seen it as an option, that somehow she thought no one would want her with it, incomplete.

I don't tell you this story because I think there's a moral in it. There isn't.

I'm on a date with a very sweet transguy. We've made out on each of our dates, and every time, I have this overpowering sensation of him having a cock. And it's not just that he's packing. It's something else, something about the way he moves against me; I keep expecting him to pull it out of his pants, or slide down my zipper and enter me. At dinner he tells me he wants bottom surgery. It's clear he's petrified of what he's just told me and terrified of my response. I tell him the truth: a few days earlier I'd been thinking that if I ever saw him naked, I'd be surprised if he didn't have a dick, since it really felt to me that he already had one. His face gets red, his eyes tear up, and he says, "No one's ever said that to me before."

I tell you these stories because, ultimately, they're about me. About my own challenge to distinguish between changing your body because you love it and changing your body because you hate it. They're about me trying to love my own body, and watching that process reflected in the people closest to me, my community. Our community is in transition. And like all our therapists tell us, it's important to be gentle with yourself during a transition. That's my wish for our community, as it were, that during this very confusing and amazing time, we be gentle with ourselves, and with each other.

Consent

When it comes to relationships, there are certain questions I ask myself: Is this what I want? Will this be enough for me? Can I accept this and let go of every other option? Each relationship is a series of questions, asked minute by minute, answered hour by hour, with touch, phone calls, favors, explicit and implicit consent to the dailyness of need.

I believe relationships and sex parties fit under the category of Be Careful What You Ask For. Not me, but you. Well, me too, I guess.

I went to a lot of sex parties in the '90s. They became a hobby—recreation—like going down the block for a beer, playing pool, tossing darts. There was a house maybe two hundred steps from where I lived that hosted Pansexual Night on Tuesdays, and I was a regular. Kind of like having my own bar stool; the owner let me in for free.

These were amazing times. One night, the eve of my birthday, I found myself at the center of a gorgeous flower, four men adoring me while being sexual with each other. For hours, these four hot men made sex and pleasure around and with me. It felt like a birthday wish come true, one that I hadn't even known to dream of.

Some of these parties were on weeknights, and some days I'd be up until 1 a.m., then show up to work at the publishing company the next morning, exhausted and energized from the connection of the night before. One unhappily married, unrealized bisexual co-worker was my confidante about my adventures. She'd listen with a ferocious, vicarious intensity that sometimes made me feel a bit guilty as I wondered what the stories might bring her to face in her own life. She wanted all the details: How did it feel the first time? How does sex get initiated?

What if you're not into it? Aren't you embarrassed to do things in front of other people?

Her most striking questions were: Doesn't it ruin it to have to talk about it? To get it once you had to ask for it? Don't you want them to just know what to do? I had told her about the negotiations that go on, in which people approach each other and ask for what they want (e.g., Can I stroke your arm? Feel like kissing? Want a massage?), and in which whole discussions about what would happen sexually—including things that wouldn't happen—often took place before any sex. I even attended a party in which the ice-breaker was a game in which we practiced saying "Yes" and "No" to touch from others across the circle from us.

"Actually, Lisa," I told her, "it's amazing to say what you want and have someone actually give it to you." There's something so rare about that, and so satisfying.

Around this time I started dating the last man I would date for more than a decade. I met him at a Jeff Buckley concert that a mutual friend, Gordon, had invited me to. (Gordon and I had met at a sex party. We had a date after the party, and right before we slept together again I found out he was married. That ended the dating, but the friendship continued.) The opening folksinger was the worst, most melodramatic, self-important performer I'd ever seen. Her lyrics included a metaphor in which she compared herself to Jesus on the cross. Oddly enough, the audience loved her. Everyone in the place was enthralled by her. Everyone except me and Paul, my friend's friend. He and I were biting our hands to keep from giggling out loud, practically peeing in our pants, convulsing with suppressed laughter. At intermission, he bought me the singer's CD.

Paul was a lawyer, fourteen years older than me, from a working class Baltimore background. He was willing to date me, even while I dated women and went to sex parties without him. He was straight, in the best sense of the word, not turned on by what I did or what it could mean for him, but turned on by me. He also wasn't turned off by it. At first. It took a big mistake on my part to turn him off, a mistake I still regret.

Paul was so in love with me and so basically nice that he was open to trying new things that he'd never really considered before. I realize that I have this messed up idea about men that they're all super sex-obsessed and willing to do anything with anyone, but somehow, all the men I've ever dated hadn't had a lot of lovers and hadn't really experimented a whole lot. I guess it's possible they could have been lying or trying to downplay, but I think the seemingly girl-next-door-with-an-inner-wild-child attracts really decent, straight but open-minded guys. After a year and half with me, Paul wore a cock ring to court when arguing a case in front of a judge and even wore fishnets under his tux at a law firm dinner. The sad thing is, I don't think I was in love with Paul. I loved him a lot and wanted to have fun.

A time came when Paul decided he wanted to go to a sex party with me. We decided we would just go and see what happened. I introduced him to friends of mine and he was welcomed warmly. I was approached by one of the guys from my birthday eve escapade. I introduced him and Paul, and then the guy asked me to play. I asked Paul if he wanted to join in. He said he'd wander around for a while and check back later. When he did come back, me and birthday guy were having sex; I can remember looking at Paul over the guy's shoulder. He looked at me from across the room but didn't come closer. When the guy and I finished, I went to find Paul. He was at the snack table, chatting with a pro-dom friend of mine as boy porn played on the TV screen overhead. Paul seemed upset, so we left.

"That was horrible," Paul said. It had been awful for him to see me with another man, and to not know how to join in, interrupt, or connect while I was playing with someone else. He hadn't known ahead of time how it would feel emotionally, and I hadn't had the foresight, nor the desire, to limit what we did until we knew how it would feel. I learned a lesson that worked well from there on out, even after Paul, which is the first time I take a partner to a sex party, I play only with them, if we play at all.

There were times when I didn't play at all. I did say "No" sometimes. I had learned my lesson. After Paul and I broke up, I dated Carly, the first person I dated who was younger than me. After my first few dates with Carly, it seemed like it might lead to a relationship, so I thought I should be honest with her about my other activities. I told her I was invited to a good-bye party for Dr. Mary, a performance artist I'd had a crush on who was leaving town. Dr. Mary was leaving town and she wanted to have sex with all the people she never had gotten to. I was one of them. I was very excited. And I was beginning a new relationship. The timing wasn't great. Carly was a one-woman kind of girl. She said she wouldn't stop me from doing what I wanted, but she wasn't sure she'd be able to stay with me either, after it was all said and done. I decided not to partake in Dr. Mary's farewell party. Well, I did go to the party, but I didn't stay long and I didn't have sex. I gave myself and the relationship a chance. That relationship is long over, and I still don't regret the choice.

The best experiences I ever had with a partner at a sex party was also my longest relationship. Spike had always dated wholesome girls who clung to her tightly. She was ready for something different, and I was a different breed entirely. Some of our best times together were having sex together with other people. We had amazing times, like the first time when—after I tied her to me, paraded her around, and let other people flog her—she fucked me in the party's basement hidey-hole area. Afterwards, we just danced and danced together to the weird piped-in music. Maybe hours went by, just the two of us—no one came in—just the two of us dancing in the dungeon surrounded by cages, crosses, chains, and leather. In those surroundings, the most perverted thing was to just romance each other, dancing.

We negotiated well and carefully before going to parties together, which most often had the result of me feeling closer to her and sweetly connected. She was brave and sexy and her taste in other people was foreign to me, in a way that most often didn't feel threatening. There was room for all of it. There was so much room that my ex is now in love with someone I introduced her to, in a sexual situation I created for her birthday while we were together.

I ran into Paul last year downtown, holding his three-year-old. The previous time I'd seen him was almost ten years ago at his wedding, when he was marrying the woman he dated after me. He was happy and content. I got that feeling I get now sometimes, that I've had a lot of amazing adventures but nothing too tangible to show for them. Not necessarily questioning my previous choices, but asking myself a different question: one dealing with commitment, focus, and intimacy. A question about freedom you want for yourself, but don't necessarily want your partner to have… about how much do you want them… and how much do they want you.

Bitter

So I'm reading Martin Luther King Jr., knowing that his words will inspire me to write something real, something starkly clear about compassion, love and hate. Something easy for a poet to understand, to grab and run with. And instead I read, "The end of violence or the aftermath of violence is bitterness." Bitterness? I was expecting something simple, like hate. Hate's an easy one, clearly not productive, not the way toward understanding, goodwill to all men—but bitterness? How can a poet not be bitter? Isn't that what we do? How can a poet avoid bitterness? Isn't bitterness the badge of the oppressed, the mark of the intellectual, the carrying card of the poet? Haven't we earned that? Isn't bitterness the birthright of every kid with parents, the severance for anyone who's ever been fired, the consolation of anyone who's ever been dumped?

Yet, despite my own resistance to peaceful resistance, I have been feeling a bit more sensitive lately. Universally tender around the edges. One of the symptoms of this new sensitivity is that I have a hard time calling the president an idiot. In September, I was at an antiwar rally among thousands of people, being yelled at through a megaphone, pelted by the force of the righteous, leftist, peaceful anger, amplified so that it could reach each and every one of us. I felt the anger and wondered how that could fix anything, how more anger and hate could ever be the answer. I began to question the everyday use of words like target, fight, battleground. And even subtler words like attacked, manipulated, abandoned.

I began to wonder how many times have I used words as weapons, loving the cunning blade of an epithet, the blunt edge of a curse, the invisible sting of the passive tense, the tiny torture of needling gossip that flies so easily from my tongue? How many words have I shaped to kill, or at least designed to cause damage? I have pages of sharp words thoughtfully crafted to exact apologies, shame, or forgiveness. So if I relinquish bitterness, how do I resist from a place of love? What words do I employ to express the pain, desperation, insistence; what kind of tone and content do I use to motivate change? How do I rebel peacefully, actively? In Martin Luther King, Jr.'s own words, be "strongly aggressive spiritually."

He calls on us to be maladjusted. He asks us to not get adjusted to segregation, discrimination, oppression. He takes the subtlest weapons of violence out of my hands and offers me agape: an overflowing love that seeks nothing in return. Agape: understanding, creative, redemptive love, he says. Spontaneously self-giving love expressed freely, the dictionary says. He hands me agape: love seeking to preserve and create community. I think of our community, connected by the sound of a word in the air. I chose the word agape, being a poet and Jew not schooled in God's love of man, but fully informed of the benefits of unconditional love. My excited mind rests on agape. Wide open. An attitude or state of wonder, expectation, or eager attention. And although I often tell myself it's not cool to be eager—it's so much more sophisticated to critique, find fault, take exception—I also find that the more I know, the more I wonder. So I roll with agape. A poet's agape is a mouth agape. A poet's mouth agape lets in as well as it releases. A mouth agape doesn't confine words that manage to escape, but rather nurtures them, gives them shape on their way out, tender letter corners bouncing like so many thistles on slick teeth and pliant lips. A poet's mouth agape invites the audience's breath in for a visit, the listener's ear takes a load off, puts up its feet on the molar coffee table. A poet's mouth agape is a powerful forceless moment, the wonderful intercourse of little words between us, unprotected, unarmed.

He speaks of disinterested love. I do not need to like you. I do not need to know what you think of my politics or my poetry. I only have to love you. I only have to offer you the best that I have.

Transition

The first girl I ever fell in love with was a punk rock dyke from Boston. Let's call her Jesse. So Jesse had this thing: she loved fucking bi girls. Not straight bi girls, but bi girls on the edge, at-risk bi girls on the precipice of being queer. Jesse had this way of asking questions, getting you to talk, and then fucking you senseless. After my ten hours with her, I cried and wrote and cried and wrote the whole way back on the plane. I had this odd, overwhelming sense that she had gotten me pregnant, with myself.

The first time I met you, we didn't kiss, but we did have breakfast the next morning before my flight. And it was in that sweet Southern lilt of yours that I first heard you refer to yourself as a homosexual female, with none of the too-cool-for-school irony I'd expect if that phrase were uttered in San Francisco. I winced as I heard the church in your words.

There's this thing I do. You could call it a predilection for distance. When it comes to love, the farther the better, or so it would seem by my habits. Suitors prove their love for me by traversing the country. I resist, albeit weakly, but it always backfires, making the phone calls, road trips, and plane fares all the more urgent.

I said no to you, but it was too late and half-hearted. How could I resist? You'd never been west of the Rockies. You'd never heard spoken word before me. You were devastatingly handsome. And you didn't have words for what no Atlanta girl had recognized in you yet.

You crossed within days. In California together, we renamed body parts. As Army Street is to César Chávez, breast became chest, clit became cock. Whole neighborhoods relocated as sex took place in previously uninhabitable homes. You got younger overnight: woman became boy, born into sweaty sheets.

And me, I played the coach, nervous chaperone, dropping you off at the gender amusement park, lips pressed tightly, knowing the dangers that lurked behind the life-sized rides, but committed to your discovery. I said nothing, save for a few encouraging words, noticing the new hair growth on your legs that you'd stopped shaving, and making a quick wish that you'd be at the park gates when I came to pick you up at the end of the day.

Within weeks, you came out as trans. "Genderqueer" fell from your lips, that week's new vocabulary word.

No one comes to San Francisco by mistake. Distant families blame the Castro or "those new friends of yours," but the tickets were bought years ago; it was just a matter of time.

Jesse dragged me, willingly and roughly, from bi-curious into queerness, my bare knees scraping the rocks I stumbled over as I crossed the river between what I was in the world and what I truly wanted to be. I understand the allure now, what it's like to sense that hunger in someone's longing gaze your way, reaching out a hand for the leap across the waters. I understand standing back a bit to avoid the splash as they jump. And I understand stepping away, walking home alone, because you can't take the journey with them.

Jesse, I get it now. I know what it's like to see something in someone that they don't see yet in themselves. I know what it's like to introduce someone into a world they've always belonged to but never knew existed. I know what it's like to fuck someone so hard they start writing poetry, turning a silent crush into a songbird.

I understand, Jesse, and I forgive you for not keeping the gift of myself that I gave you. Because I understand now how much easier, how much more pleasurable it is to focus on someone else's transition than your own.

Condition

It took quite a while to get here, delays and cancellations, unexpected late-night layover in a rainy city. But I made it to Iowa in time to kick off the Pride Week celebration at Grinnell College. Grinnell, jewel of the prairie.

It took a long time to get here, talking about intersex in Iowa. More than seven years, many plane flights, missteps, and friendships across the map. I heard from two such people since I began the trip to Iowa two days ago, angry and hurt about the term DSDs, disorders of sex development, being used by some intersex advocates.

I'm lonely in Iowa. The wind's a constant reminder of nothing outside the window but grass, a couple of trailers, and train tracks as far as the eye can see. The town of Grinnell has many American cars and no parking meters, two railroad lines, and wireless Internet at one café. No one locks their bike. No rockstar myself, I still stick out in my black jacket against the fluorescent T-shirts and pastels. It was recently Easter, after all.

There's a picture of my mom and me on the cover of the ISNA parents' handbook. Standing out, risking community for the sake of showing parents and doctors that intersex people are whole human beings, not just naked bodies with eyes blackened out for privacy's sake.

There are rolling hills, but it's still so flat. I feel so round and so curly here, where hermaphrodite is used more often than intersex, where the one intersex student I've met doesn't like that word either.

A long time ago I didn't think I was intersex, then intersex people told me I was. There were those that didn't trust me because I hadn't had surgery, and there were those that didn't trust me because I talked about sex too openly. Always there were those so desperate for community that any disagreement was seen as a threat. Always, there were those who knew there are far too few of us.

Being in Iowa—Grinnell, Iowa—is being on an island. An hour from the closest mall. I never knew a mall could mean safety and community, but that's the world we live in.

How far we have to travel sometimes to see ourselves reflected. How far we have to travel from ourselves.

A trans activist tells me that using the word "disorder" pathologizes us. I tell her it's nothing compared to what they already call us. I was at a medical conference in Arizona, in a room full of pediatric urologists and endocrinologists who gave a standing ovation to a woman who announced that her daughter had Congenital Adrenal Hyperplasia but she wasn't intersex, her daughter wasn't a freak.

Look, I told the activist, even the word "variation" wouldn't past muster with these doctors. There are those working for a new framework, for paths to trans and intersex treatment options that don't pathologize. But, in the meantime, doctors are doing irreversible cosmetic surgeries on five babies a day. In the meantime, I know an intersex kid who underwent normalizing surgery as a baby, who was raised without information about her body and her surgery until very recently, and this kid is angry and dangerously suicidal. There are activists working to depathologize pathologization. And that's how I see it: if our bodies are disordered in some way, they may need medical care, but they don't need medicalization. I want medical care that seeks to make me happy, not to make me normal.

I believe in speaking to people in language they'll understand. I've got CAH when I talk to doctors; I'm intersex when I talk to activists; I've got a medical condition when I talk to my boss.

After all these years in the intersex community, I can tell you there is no intersex community. There's a bunch of people who have a variety of bodies, some radically different from each other, and even more different experiences. What many of us have in common are repeated genital displays, often from a young age. Many of us have had medical treatments done to us without our consent to make our sex anatomy conform to someone else's standards. Many of us suffer from intense shame due to treatments that sought to fix or hide our bodies. And many of us have experienced none of the above.

Some of us have more in common with fat people than with each other. Some of us have more in common with disabled people than each other. And many of us have a lot in common with sexual abuse survivors.

Each time I leave my smoke-free motel room and enter the long, smoke-filled hallway, I pass the front desk and a fighting fish, midnight and motionless in the empty-but-for-the-black-and-blue-marbles water-filled bowl. A clear plastic pot that probably once held flowers rests above him on the rim of the bowl. I check on him each time I walk by, and each time he's just floating there, on his side. I wonder if I'm the only person who notices and each time I try not to look, but he's slow roadkill from someone's birthday and I can't stop myself, compulsively checking on his condition.

Finally, upon checkout, I can stand it no longer. "I think that fish is having a tough time," I tell the guy.

"Looks like Fluffy's on his last legs," he shouts over to his co-worker in the back office. And I feel so much better.

Okay

I wish my mom had known how smart she was

I wish my mom had known that grief is too heavy a burden to carry on your own

I wish my mom had known that congenital adrenal hyperplasia was a gift that would make me an outsider, a community organizer, a runner, and a writer

I wish my mom had known that doctors don't know everything

I wish my mom had known that despite what my dad said, it was okay to talk about what was happening and that she deserved support

I wish my mom had known that doing everything in her power to make me normal wouldn't make me normal

I wish my mom had known that I knew how upset she was, and that I thought it was my fault

I wish my mom had known that facial hair on a girl isn't the worst thing

I wish my mom had known it was okay that I was curious about sex before other kids

I wish my mom had known that it's not helpful to put a kid on the Scarsdale Diet even if doctors tell you your child needs to lose weight

I wish my mom had known that by raising me to be proud of myself, she gave me confidence to accept myself as different

I wish my mom had known that I needed support because being different is hard, even under the best circumstances

I wish my mom had known that accepting myself as different was the key to realizing that everyone in the world feels different

I wish my mom had known that calling myself intersex would be the key I needed to meet others like me, to see myself reflected, and to heal my shame

I wish my mom had known that there would be a community for me, people who would accept me just as I am, people who would consider me a teacher, a leader, an ideal lover, and people who would feel that by being myself I offer others a safe haven, a nest at the top of the tallest lonely tree

I wish my mom had known that more than thirty years after my diagnosis, she would fall into the arms of a dancing man that wasn't my father, and that she would finally cry her heart out

And that we would both be okay

More than okay

Hope

I'm looking for the war inside. I'm going in. Cover me.

There are so many wars. On prisoners, drug users, the poor, the environment. What's your darling war of the moment? I'd say that sometimes it's hard to leave the house, but if you're paying attention at all you don't even need to leave the house to learn more than you want to know.

I'm speaking to you—you, who live in Iowa or the Mission; you, who watch TV, get glimpses of the horrors in short phrases on your Yahoo! home page; you, who read blogs from Asia, Eastern Europe, Iraq. I don't have to name the horrors of waking up. You're awake, and you hurt, too.

Times like these, it's especially important to talk to older people. Older older. Does it always feel like the world is ending? That it's destroying itself? Nothing to me is scarier than an old person who tells you it's worse than it's ever been.

My best friend said yesterday that she thinks we're ending. Not her and me. Humans. That our time is ending. To make room for something new. She said it takes a lot of faith to have kids these days. Not that she's ever wanted them.

Where do you find hope?

I say that woman at my job is really annoying because I don't think she's being real. A tiny bullet. I call my neighbor irresponsible for drinking and driving. Another bullet. I tell you I'm a loser for not going to that party. A grenade, undetonated maybe, but destructive all the same.

I find hope in language.

Sometimes I say that I feel nervous when I work with that woman at my job because I value authenticity and want to know we're connected when we work together. Sometimes I say I'm scared when my neighbor drinks and drives because I want her to be safe. Sometimes I say I feel anxious because I want to make a contribution and I want acceptance for my choices and for who I am in the world... mostly from myself.

You say you get embarrassed sometimes because you haven't made anything of yourself. If I could draw kindness, I'd color up and down your arms, a cacophony of good morning in Cantonese, of pictures taped to the seat backs in the school bus to keep the kids from fighting, of infinitely strong hands that live only to serve, all sorts of magic that turns little wars into laughter.

Be gentle, I say, and be careful. Meaning too often turns against itself, turns inward. Career means an excuse for imbalance. Wealth is a poverty of imagination. Success is a sword that hardly ever leads to happiness.

I find hope in the space between you and me, and between me and my self.

I hope that peace becomes a household word. Echoing inside me and emanating from you, a trusty lighthouse on the seven seas.

C/leaving

Yes, there are wild geese
Those for whom life passes like the seasons
Smooth and without question
And then there are the rest of us

We plant apple trees, but never eat the fruit
We are the ones who dream, but don't believe
We'll actually ever get there,
Thirty a vanishing point, Forty an inside joke
An endless road trip, torn map, abandoned farm

It is not for me to judge where we live
The thing that got my dad into prison is
The same thing that will get him out
There is no illegal, no wrong
We never were right

We met at the corner of mourning and heartbreak
In your small car you showed me your darkness
Like unbuttoning your shirt, but more naked
A gift black box wrapped in words

You told me
Leaving is the only power
We lived through winter and grew apart in spring
I never opened it again

I used to wear a silver ring on each thumb
Marking queerness
Words stamped in the soft metal: question and accept
There is the daily work of acceptance

Choice, the deepest kind
Is an illusion I use
To soothe myself to sleep
Daily

There is the ground
The soil
And the question of
What to do with these hands

Acknowledgments

First and foremost, thank you to Jen Joseph of Manic D Press, for always understanding my voice and believing in my work. Much gratitude goes to Greg Wharton and Ian Philips who kept telling me "Just write a beautiful book" and then helped me do just that.

Much appreciation to my family, who have decided it's better to not be mentioned in one of Thea's books and yet still let me. Without their support, what would I have to rebel against?

Huge thanks to the this book's initial readers: Justin Chin, Storm Florez, Diane Fraser, Tamar Hurwitz, Danna James, and Kendra Lubalin, who all pretty much told me the that regardless of what I thought I was writing, the book was about intersex.

Many of the pieces in this book are a result of performances I've been invited to participate in or curate, so big thanks are due to Sam Davis, Sean Dorsey, Michelle Tea, Pam Peniston, the Queer Cultural Center, and the folks at Jon Sims Center for the Performing Arts.

Love and many thanks to Cheryl Chase, Bo Laurent, Alice Dreger, the ISNA board members, the activists, my intersex friends, my friends with DSDs, and those who trusted me enough to come to me with questions about the scars they know very little or nothing about.

Finally, thanks to everyone who created these stories by living them with me. Especially the lovers, whose trust is no small thing and who were brave more than once.

About the Author

An award-winning author and former San Francisco Poetry Slam Champion, Thea Hillman received an MFA in Creative Writing from Mills College. She has produced and co-produced national tours and performance events including *ForWord Girls*, *Shameless*, *Rated XXXY*, *Intercourse*, and *Hell on Heels*.

Thea Hillman served on the Board of Mills College and as chair of the Board of the Intersex Society of North America. She performs her work around the country, and presents informational talks and spoken word performances about intersex and activism. The author of the critically acclaimed *Depending on the Light*, this is Hillman's second book. Visit Thea Hillman online: www.theahillman.com